THIRD EYE ESP

Harnessing Psychic Powers for
Success Through Ancient Indian
Practices and Wisdom

Mohd Faisal

M. Faisal Publications

"The Universe is not outside of you. Look inside yourself; everything that you want, you already are."

– RUMI

CONTENTS

PROLOGUE

A force as old as time itself exists in the domain of human potential. It is a deep and mysterious power. This ability is inherent in each and every one of us and extends beyond the confines of the material world. It is the Third Eye, latent yet ever-powerful.

With all of the noise in our life these days and the never-ending rush of our daily schedules, we often forget about the limitless potential we all possess. The wise counsel of our forefathers, the mystics and sages who transcribed the universe's mysteries into the wind and inscribed their wisdom on the fabric of antiquated Indian customs, has been lost to us.

But there's a call, hidden deep within us, in the quiet murmurs of lost customs, the echoes of faraway memories, and the unsaid truths: a summons to open the Third Eye, to activate latent psychic talents, and to set out on a path of spiritual and personal development.

Your path to this deep awakening is this book, "Third Eye ESP: Harnessing Psychic Powers for Success Through Ancient Indian Practices and Wisdom." We are going to go together to the hitherto unexplored regions of human awareness.

The Third Eye's mysteries will be revealed to you as you read the pages that follow. You will learn about the rich tradition of ancient Indian knowledge and the mystical teachings that have guided searchers for years. We will explore the power of the chakras, awaken the serpentine energy of Kundalini, and navigate the maze-like paths of meditation and visualization.

You will explore the areas of intuition, telepathy, telekinesis, and clairvoyance and discover how to use these remarkable abilities. However, our adventure doesn't end there. We will explore the unexplored fields of remote viewing, astral projection, and out-of-body experiences.

You will learn how to use these psychic abilities to alter yourself on a personal level as well as to improve your relationships, advance your job, take better care of yourself, and finally succeed beyond all expectations.

But we must not lose sight of the significance of ethics and integrity as we make our way through this enormous journey. tremendous power with a tremendous deal of responsibility. We'll talk about the moral applications of third-eye abilities and how you might utilize your abilities to improve the world.

We shall be thoroughly immersed in the knowledge of contemporary mystics, ancient sages, and common practitioners who have developed their Third Eyes and used their psychic abilities to achieve extraordinary success in each chapter. Their experiences will act as inspirational lighthouses, lighting your path and directing you in the direction of your own awakening.

You have been carrying around the Third Eye, waiting for the right opportunity to activate it. Now is the moment to answer its call, solve its puzzles, and set forth on a voyage of seemingly endless possibilities. Your instruments on your journey to enlightenment are the counsel found in these pages and the wisdom of the ancients.

Are you prepared to awaken the latent potential inside yourself?

Are you ready to use your psychic abilities and use your Third Eye to live a successful, exciting, and limitless life? If yes, let's get started on our voyage.

CHAPTER 1: THE MYSTICAL THIRD EYE UNVEILED

The third eye is a dazzling diamond that draws us with its mystery in the realms of spirituality and the occult. This idea, which is firmly woven within Hinduism's fabric, serves as a doorway to unseen realities. It's a portal to a world beyond the ordinary, a realm that extends beyond the confines of our daily lives.

How does this 'third eye' work? Is it the stuff of tales or a real element of who we are?

1. The Third Eye Concept

Imagine it as an inner eye, lightly poised between your brows on your forehead. This eye is made of energy and awareness rather than flesh and blood. It is known as the 'Ajna' or 'Anja' chakra in Hinduism, and it is very important in the practice of yoga and meditation.

The third eye is more than just an abstract concept; it is an ancient and holy symbol that signifies the meeting of our inner and outside worlds. It's a link between the everyday and the magical, the tangible and the metaphysical.

Cross-Cultural Views on the Third Eye

While Hinduism is definitely the birthplace of the third eye idea, it is important to recognize that it transcends cultural borders. The concept of a 'third eye' or inner vision existed in numerous civilizations in various forms and under various names.

The ancient Egyptians, for example, presented their deity Horus with a third eye, indicating his omnipotence and enhanced vision. This mystical eye appears on the Dharma Wheel in Buddhism, representing spiritual insight and enlightenment.

It is a worldwide emblem of greater awareness and spiritual awakening, with an impact that extends well beyond the confines of any one religion or belief system. Whether you name it the third eye, the inner eye, or something else completely, its mystique connects us all.

The Power Of Esp

Imagine a place in which the mind spreads its wings and flies beyond the known world's limitations. It's a world where information travels in whispers, ideas fly, and sensations stretch beyond the bounds of our physical senses. This is the ethereal world of Extra-Sensory Perception, or simply ESP.

Let us go on an incredible adventure, where conventional laws of vision no longer apply and your mind's eye becomes a beacon of untapped potential.

Exploring Extra-Sensory Perception (ESP)

ESP, which conjures up visions of mystics and psychics, is the skill of seeing via unusual ways. It is the amazing capacity to see beyond what the eye can perceive, hear what sound cannot, and feel the intangible. ESP is not magic, but rather an expression of the human psyche's boundless powers.

It incorporates a plethora of remarkable senses, such as telepathy, clairvoyance, precognition, and psychometry, each of which demonstrates the limitless capacity of the human mind. In this chapter, we'll set sail into new territory, exploring the depths of the mind's possibilities.

The Role of ESP in Personal and Professional Success

This is where things get interesting. The enigmatic realm of ESP is more than simply a curiosity for those who are fascinated by the mysterious. It's a power that may light up both your personal and professional life. Your natural capacity to access ESP might be the key to opening previously locked doors.

In your personal life, ESP may serve as a guidepost for your relationships and decisions. Consider the ability to connect with loved ones on a deep, intuitive level, or experiencing flashes of insight that indicate the route to happiness.

In the professional sphere, ESP becomes your hidden weapon, a tool that improves decision-making and problem-solving. The whisper of inspiration inspires invention and creativity, and the edge that separates success from mediocrity.

Whether you're an artist, a scientist, a healer, or a business leader, the power of ESP has the ability to drive you to unexplored heights. The voyage of discovery starts with acknowledging its presence, and with each step ahead, you'll learn the significant influence it may have on your life.

2. Ancient Indian Wisdom

Enter a world where time moves like a sage's footsteps and knowledge flows like a holy river. It's a world where spirituality isn't just an idea, but a live, breathing force woven into the fabric of existence. Welcome to the core of ancient Indian knowledge, a treasury of enlightenment and the basis for third eye activation.

The Rich Spiritual Heritage of India

India, a country steeped in history, echoes with the footsteps of many seekers who traveled into the realm of the sublime. This ancient land's spiritual tradition is a tapestry woven with strands of meditation, devotion, and deep understanding. From the towering Himalayas to the tranquil banks of the Ganges, India's holy terrain reflects the breadth of its spiritual past.

India's knowledge is more than just books and temples; it is a living, breathing creature. It's in the aroma of incense drifting through the air, the sounds of bhajans sung at nightfall, and the wind's whispers as it caresses the banyan tree's leaves.

Yoga and Meditation: The Foundation of Third Eye Activation

If you were to go deep into Indian spirituality, you would surely end yourself on the road of yoga and meditation. These ancient techniques are more than just exercises; they are portals to the soul, keys to awakening the buried potential inside. Meditation is a voyage inside, a trek to the heart of your being, whereas yoga is the integration of mind, body, and spirit.

Yoga, with its many postures and breathing practices, prepares the body and mind for higher levels of awareness. It is the vehicle that will transport you to the beaches of meditation, where the third eye will awaken.

We'll dig into the art of yoga and the essence of meditation in this chapter, unraveling their mystery and investigating the significant influence they have on third eye activation. From pranayama to asanas, from the lotus posture to the holy 'Om,' we'll walk the ancient paths that lead to the third eye opening.

So, whether you're a seasoned yogi or a curious newcomer, come along with us as we explore ancient Indian knowledge, where the past and present collide and the third eye awaits its revelation.

4. Meditation And Visualization Techniques

Meditation is a spiritual journey into the undiscovered realms of the mind in the domain of inner discovery. It's a quiet dialogue with your own spirit, a trip in which you are both the passenger and the destination. Among the many types of meditation, mindfulness meditation stands out as a source of enlightenment.

Mindfulness Meditation Practice

For a minute, close your eyes and picture yourself in a tranquil garden. It's not just any garden; it's your awareness' garden. Every idea, emotion, and feeling is like a flower or a tree swinging in the wind. This is what mindfulness meditation is all about.

Mindfulness Meditation is the practice of being totally present in the moment, of watching your thoughts and sensations as they change without judgment. It's about embracing the present moment, recognizing it, and allowing it to pass like the movement of a river.

To meditate on awareness, locate a peaceful place where you won't be interrupted. Sit in a comfortable position, with your spine straight and your hands on your lap. Close your eyes gently. Take a deep breath in and exhale to release any tension in your body.

Now concentrate on your breathing. Feel the feeling of your breath entering and exiting your body. With each breath, pay attention to the rise and fall of your chest or the movement of your belly. Breathe naturally without attempting to regulate it.

Thoughts will surely come while you sit in silence. It's a component of the human condition. Rather of battling these ideas, embrace them. Recognize them when they arise, and then restore your attention to your breathing. Consider writing each idea on a leaf and letting it float away on the river of your mind.

It's totally normal for your thoughts to stray from time to time. Mindfulness meditation is a discipline, and it gets easier to sustain attention with time. Be kind with yourself; there is no hurry.

Begin with short sessions, maybe five or ten minutes, and gradually increase the time as you grow more used to the practice. Mindfulness meditation may gradually open the door to the domain of the third eye, improving perception and inner awareness.

As you continue your voyage of discovery, keep in mind that mindfulness meditation is a powerful key to unlocking the secrets of your mind, clearing the path for deeper levels of awareness and the waking of your third eye.Trataka for Third Eye Activation

Trataka is a fascinating note in the symphony of third eye activation, harmonizing with the vibrations of ancient knowledge and concentrated attention. This yoga practice invites you to look deeply into the worlds of your own awareness, enabling the third eye to open.

Trataka, which translates to "steady gazing," is a time-honored method that has been venerated for ages. It is the practice of focusing one's attention on a single point, usually a candle flame or a symbol, in order to sharpen one's intellect and increase the strength of one's inner vision.

To begin this adventure, choose a peaceful place and sit comfortably. Place a bright candle or an item with a clear sign approximately a meter or so distant from your eyes. Maintain your gaze on the thing without blinking for as long as you can comfortably handle.

While gazing, your mind may wander through ideas and diversions. That is understandable. When this occurs, gently bring your attention back to the thing. The flame or symbol becomes your anchor, and the third eye wakes in this quiet.

Trataka not only improves focus and mental clarity, but it also serves as a catalyst for the activation of the third eye. Your intuitive and psychic skills may become more evident with continuous practice.

Visualization for ESP Enhancement

Imagination serves as the canvas for the most profound alterations. Visualization becomes the brush that paints the rich landscapes of your inner world in the region of third eye activation. It's the key to uncovering the secrets of your awareness and improving your Extra-Sensory Perception (ESP).

Begin this exercise by locating a quiet, peaceful place that is devoid of distractions. Close your eyes, take a few deep breaths, and let the stresses of the day wash over you. As you relax, see your third eye as a dazzling, indigo-colored lotus in the middle of your forehead

Imagine the petals of this lotus gently opening, exposing a bright, cosmic eye at its heart. As the eye opens, imagine it emitting an ethereal light that illuminates the darkness of the unknown.

At this point, let your thoughts roam into this inner dimension. Imagine your intuitive senses waking up. Visualize yourself getting insights, pictures, and knowledge from inside your being. Trust the process and be open to whatever surprises come your way.

With time and dedication, this technique may sharpen your intuition, making the intangible more obvious. The third eye, or inner eye, becomes a lighthouse that leads you into unexplored perceptual territory.

Breathing Exercises for Energy Alignment

The breath, a seemingly insignificant energy that keeps us alive, also contains the key to unlocking the power of the third eye.

You may balance your energies and lay the basis for intuitive awakening by using conscious, purposeful breathwork.

Sit in a relaxed posture with your spine straight and your hands on your lap. Take a few deep, cleansing breaths while closing your eyes. Release whatever stress you may be carrying as you exhale.

Now concentrate on your breathing. Allow your abdomen to lift as you inhale deeply. Feel the discharge of any stagnant or bad energy as you breath. Continue to breathe rhythmically, allowing your breath to become a constant, relaxing presence.

Imagine pulling in pure, brilliant light as you breathe in. This light pervades your whole body, from the top of your head to the soles of your feet. Visualize any weight, tension, or negativity exiting your body as black smoke as you exhale.

You're flooding your body with vivid, positive energy with each inhale. With each exhale, you remove any impediments to your energy flow. This technique not only cleanses your energy, but it also aligns it with the higher frequencies required for third-eye activation.

By doing these breathing exercises, your inner eye becomes more sensitive, aware, and active, allowing you to enter a realm where your consciousness transcends the ordinary and dives into the exceptional.

CHAPTER 2: THE SCIENCE AND SPIRITUALITY OF THE THIRD EYE

1. The Pineal Gland: The Physical Third Eye

A small, pinecone-shaped gland deep beneath the delicate folds of your brain has been heralded as the physical expression of the third eye. The pineal gland, a fascinating gland, is a meeting point between science and spirituality, a meeting point between the physical and the metaphysical.

In the scientific world, the pineal gland, about the size of a grain of rice, plays a critical role in regulating our sleep-wake cycles via melatonin release. However, it is in the realms of spirituality and mysticism that this gland is known as the "seat of the soul" and the "physical third eye."

The connection between the pineal gland and the third eye is not only metaphorical; it is firmly anchored in the anatomy and function of the pineal gland. This mysterious gland contains photoreceptor cells identical to those found in the retina of the eye, making it light sensitive. It is sometimes referred to as the "third eye" because to its role in light-sensitive processes.

Throughout history, the pineal gland has been revered as the key to attaining higher states of awareness. It is seen as the link between the physical and spiritual realms in esoteric religions. The pineal gland is said to be intimately tied to the third eye chakra, or Ajna chakra, with the opening and activity of the third eye typically correlated with the stimulation of this gland.

The pineal gland, a scientific wonder buried in our brain, embodies the logical and the mystical, providing a fascinating look into the fundamental relationship between our physical bodies and our spiritual identity. The pineal gland emerges as a vital role in the search for heightened awareness and inner awakening as we explore further into the science and theology of the third eye.

Scientific Insights into the Pineal Gland

The pineal gland, sometimes known as the "seat of the soul"

and the "physical third eye," has long captivated scientists and researchers. This little pinecone-shaped gland, situated deep inside the brain, occupies a special position in biology and mysticism. Modern science has shed light on its roles and importance in recent years, uncovering some of its secrets.

1. Melatonin Synthesis:

One of the pineal gland's key roles is the creation and release of melatonin, a hormone that regulates our circadian cycles. Melatonin is essential for keeping our biological clock in line with the natural light-dark cycle. It is produced in reaction to darkness, assisting us in sleeping, and its production diminishes throughout the day.

2. Light Sensitivity:

Photoreceptor cells in the pineal gland are strikingly similar to those seen in the retina of the eye. These cells are light sensitive, and when exposed to light or darkness, they send a signal to the gland, causing it to regulate melatonin output. Because of its sensitivity to light, the pineal gland has been associated with the idea of the "third eye," since it reacts to ambient light and darkness.

3. Biological Clock Control:

The pineal gland regulates our internal biological clock by managing melatonin synthesis. This internal clock affects not just our sleep patterns, but also a variety of physiological and behavioral functions such as body temperature, hormone release, and metabolic metabolism.

4. The Role of Seasonal Changes:

The pineal gland is also involved in seasonal adaptations and is sensitive to variations in daylight duration. This sensitivity may affect seasonal behaviors and emotions in animals and, to a lesser degree, humans.

5. Affiliation with Spiritual and Mystic Traditions:

In spiritual and esoteric traditions, the pineal gland has been associated with higher consciousness and altered states of awareness, in addition to its physiological activities. Some beliefs claim that the pineal gland may have a role in enhancing spiritual experiences, while scientific study on this topic is limited.

In conclusion, although much is known about the pineal gland's physiological functioning, it remains a topic of continuous scientific investigation, especially in terms of its possible connections to spiritual and metaphysical experiences. Its dual function as a biological timekeeper and a symbol of inner awakening exemplifies the fascinating junction of science and spirituality.

2. Chakras And Energy Centers

The notion of chakras and energy centers weaves a colorful, complex pattern into the broad fabric of the human experience. This ancient concept, steeped in Indian spiritual traditions, sheds light on the interdependence of the physical and spiritual worlds. The deep knowledge of the chakras, like spinning wheels of energy that feed our life, is at the center of this system.

Understanding the Chakra System:

Imagine your body as a harmonic symphony of energy centers, each pulsing at its own distinct frequency. These energy vortexes, known as chakras, reside along the central channel of your body, from the base of your spine to the top of your head.

There are seven main chakras in all, each with its own set of physical, emotional, and spiritual characteristics. These are the energy centers:

1. Root Chakra (Muladhara):

मूलाधार चक्र

The root chakra, located near the base of the spine, signifies our basis and connection to the physical world. It influences our sentiments of safety and security, as well as our fundamental survival requirements.

2. The sacral chakra (Svadhisthana):

It is associated with our emotions, creativity, and sexuality. It is located in the lower belly. It is the source of our aspirations and passions.

3. The solar plexus chakra (Manipura)

It is located in the upper belly and is the seat of our own strength and self-esteem. It has an impact on our self-esteem and confidence.

4. The heart chakra (Anahata)

It is related with love, compassion, and emotional equilibrium. It is located at the center of the body. It is where we discover our ability to empathize and connect with others.

5. The throat chakra (Vishuddha)

It controls communication and self-expression and is located in the throat. It is the medium through which we express our ideas and emotions.

6. Third Eye Chakra (Ajna):

It is located between the brows, the third eye chakra is often associated with intuition and inner perception. It is linked to the pineal gland, often known as the "seat of the soul."

7. Crown Chakra (Sahasrara):

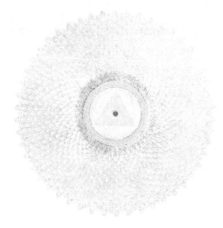

The crown chakra, located in the crown of the head, connects us to global, divine energy. It represents spiritual enlightenment and the unity of all things.

The chakra system, which is at the heart of Indian spiritual philosophy, tells us that these energy centers must be balanced and open in order for us to enjoy physical, emotional, and spiritual well-being. When these chakras are in equilibrium, they spin like perfectly balanced wheels, enabling prana, or life force energy, to flow freely.

Throughout your trip, you'll delve into each chakra's distinct traits, instabilities, and ways for balancing and harmonizing these critical places. The chakras are portals to self-awareness, development, and comprehension of the tremendous connection that exists between your physical self and the cosmos that surrounds you.

Balancing Chakras for Enhanced Perception

Balance is the melody that leads to harmony in the complicated dance of life. When it comes to chakras, finding balance is the key to unlocking heightened awareness in both the physical and spiritual worlds. Chakra balancing is an art that involves comprehension, purpose, and practice.

Consider your chakras to be spinning plates, each representing a distinct part of your physical, emotional, and spiritual health. These plates resound in perfect harmony when they spin at the correct pace. When one or more chakras become blocked or hyperactive, the symphony breaks down, resulting in imbalances in your life.

Here's how you may begin the process of chakra balancing for improved perception:

1. Muladhara (Root Chakra):

The root chakra, located near the base of the spine, is related with your feeling of safety and security. Spend time in nature, do grounding exercises, and picture a deep, crimson glow at the base of your spine to balance it.

2. Svadhisthana (Sacral Chakra):

Your creativity and emotions are governed by the sacral chakra, which is located in the lower belly. Engage in creative activities, develop emotional awareness, and envision a warm, orange glow in your lower abdomen to balance it.

3. Manipura Chakra (Solar Plexus):

The solar plexus chakra, located in the upper belly, boosts your self-esteem and personal strength. Focus on self-confidence exercises, healthy limits, and visualizing a beautiful, yellow light in your solar plexus to balance it.

4. Anahata (heart chakra):

The heart chakra, located in the heart core, is a source of love and compassion. To counteract it, do acts of kindness, cultivate healthy connections, and see a brilliant, green light in your heart.

5. Vishuddha (Throat Chakra):

The throat chakra, which is located in the throat, is associated with communication and self-expression. To counteract it, express yourself honestly, listen actively, and envision a calming blue light at your neck.

6. Ajna (Third Eye Chakra):

Intuition and inner vision are related with the third eye chakra, which is located between the brows. To counteract it, meditate, develop awareness, and picture an azure light in your third eye.

7. Sahasrara (Crown Chakra):

The crown chakra, located at the crown of the head, links you to divine and universal energy. To counteract it, engage in spiritual activities, express appreciation, and envision a brilliant, violet light at your crown.

Balancing the chakras is an ongoing process since life events may continually alter their harmony. You may nurture balance and alignment by concentrating on each chakra, learning its features, and applying visualization and mindfulness methods, resulting in heightened perception and a deeper connection to the world inside and around you.

Third Eye Activation and the Sixth Chakra:
The sixth chakra, or Ajna chakra, is a mystical doorway to greater vision and inner knowledge inside the complicated network of energy centers known as the chakras. This ethereal portal, situated between your physical eyes, is known as the "third eye." Activating the third eye and balancing the sixth chakra is a deep journey of waking your inner vision.

The third eye, symbolized as an indigo or deep blue lotus with two petals, contains the key to improved perception, intuition, and a greater knowledge of oneself and the cosmos.

Third Eye Activation:

The process of activating your inner vision and extending your perspective beyond the physical sphere is known as third eye activation. This activation comprises increased awareness, deep insights, and the capacity to see and experience things that are not visible to the naked eye.

Consider the following methods to help you open your third eye:

1. Meditation is the foundation of third eye activation. You may boost the energy of the sixth chakra by concentrating your concentration on the place between your brows. During meditation, visualization, guided imagery, and focused breathing may all help.

2. Mindful Living: Incorporate awareness into your everyday routine. Be totally present in the moment and become aware of your thoughts and sensations. This attentiveness opens the door to deeper third-eye observations.

3. Developing Intuition: Believe on your gut instincts and inner understanding. You are enhancing the abilities of your third eye as you build your intuition.

4. Keep a dream notebook and pay attention to your dreams. The dream world is inextricably linked to the third eye and may provide vital insights and symbols.

5. Engage in energy healing treatments such as Reiki or acupuncture to help remove blockages and regulate the flow of energy in the sixth chakra.

Bringing the Sixth Chakra into Balance:

The sixth chakra, the third eye, must be balanced for clarity, intuition, and awareness. It develops a deep connection with your inner self and the broader cosmos when it is in harmony. Here are some techniques for maintaining this balance:

1. Visualization: Visualize the blue light of the third eye chakra on a regular basis. Consider it brightening and expanding, offering insight and clarity.

2. Clearing Blockages: Remove emotional and mental impediments to your vision. Maintaining a clean third eye requires forgiveness, self-reflection, and letting go of attachments.

3. Participate in holistic techniques such as yoga, tai chi, or Qi Gong. These exercises not only improve physical health but also encourage energy flow via the chakras.

4. Diet and Nutrition: Eat foods that support the pineal gland and third eye, such as dark leafy greens, raw cacao, and antioxidant-rich meals.

By combining these techniques into your everyday life and feeding the sixth chakra, you may unleash the full potential of your third eye, resulting in increased perception, intuitive insights, and a stronger connection to the spiritual elements of reality.

3. Kundalini Awakening:

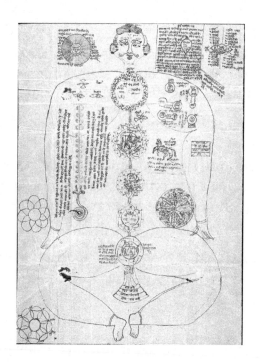

The Serpent Energy:

Kundalini awakening, commonly depicted as a coiled snake, is a deep and transforming journey within the wide domain of spirituality and inner change. It is an examination of the inner self, a journey to unlock the hidden potential that exists inside each person, and an awakening to a higher level of awareness.

The Serpent Power:

The notion of the snake energy, coiled at the base of the spine, ready to climb and light the chakras along the central channel, lies at the core of Kundalini awakening. This serpent, commonly represented as a coiled snake, signifies our latent potential.

The name "Kundalini" comes from the Sanskrit words "kundala," which means "coiled," and "kundal," which means "to burn." This strong force, like a coiled snake, is said to hold the universe's vast creative and spiritual power.

The Kundalini awakening journey entails the uncoiling and ascent of this latent energy from the base of the spine to the crown of the skull. This process is often characterized as a powerful and transforming experience that leads to spiritual enlightenment and increased awareness.

How to Awaken Your Kundalini:

Kundalini awakening is a profound and sometimes difficult process that needs devotion, practice, and a deep connection to one's inner self. The following phases are typical of the journey

1. Kundalini awakening may occur naturally or with specialized techniques such as yoga, meditation, or breathwork. It often starts with a powerful inner calling or awakening that leads people to investigate their spiritual depths.

2. Activation: As the Kundalini energy at the base of the spine awakens, people may feel physical sensations, emotional releases, and heightened awareness. This period may be accompanied by a variety of feelings, including strong heat and energy surges, as well as emotional ups and downs.

3. Ascension: As the snake energy ascends via the body's core channel, it activates and cleanses each chakra, releasing their potential and increasing consciousness. This ascension is often characterized as a great rush of energy and altered states of awareness.

4. Individuals may experience great insight, happiness, and altered states of consciousness throughout the integration process. These encounters must be incorporated into one's everyday existence in order to achieve a more balanced and enlightened state of being.

It is critical to understand that Kundalini awakening is a very personal and transforming process. While it may lead to spiritual progress and enlightenment, it can also be accompanied with physical and emotional obstacles. During this process, guidance from experienced spiritual instructors or mentors may be beneficial.

Kundalini awakening, with its coiled snake symbolism, indicates within each of us the capacity to transcend the mundane and discover the extraordinary elements of our life. It is an invitation to go inside, uncoil the dormant force, and awaken to a higher level of awareness and self-realization.

Raising Kundalini for Spiritual Enlightenment

Kundalini awakening is a potent road to spiritual enlightenment, a journey that reveals the deepest levels of the self and takes you closer to the fundamental truths of life. Raising Kundalini for spiritual enlightenment is a transforming process that involves commitment, inner investigation, and a deep connection to the divine within. Here's a checklist to help you get started on your important quest:

1. Develop Inner Awareness:

The path to Kundalini awakening starts with self-awareness. To better comprehend your inner landscape, engage in techniques such as meditation, mindfulness, and self-reflection. Self-awareness is the basis upon which Kundalini awakening is based.

2. Cleanse Your Energy

Purification is necessary for preparing your energy pathways for Kundalini's ascension. Engage in cleansing rituals for the body, mind, and soul. Adopting a good diet, keeping emotional equilibrium, and practicing forgiveness and appreciation are all examples.

3. Grounding and Centering:

Before raising Kundalini, make certain you are grounded and balanced. Grounding techniques, such as connecting with the Earth, serve to build a firm basis for energy to flow in a harmonic manner.

4. Chakra Activation

The chakras are the energy centers via which Kundalini ascends. Through meditation, visualization, and energy healing, work on balancing and activating each chakra, from the root to the crown.

5. Kundalini Yoga:

Participate in Kundalini yoga, a practice developed expressly to awaken and increase Kundalini energy. These yoga postures, breathwork, and meditation practices are designed to awaken latent power inside.

6. Pranayama (breathing exercises):

Pranayama exercises may assist in stimulating and directing the flow of Kundalini energy. Controlled breathing methods, such as Bhastrika and Nadi Shodhana, may help with this process.

7. Mantra and Sound:

Mantras and sound vibrations have the ability to stimulate Kundalini. Chanting certain mantras or listening to sound frequencies that resonate with the chakras may help.

8. Submit to the Divine:

Kundalini awakening is a profoundly spiritual event. Surrender to the almighty and have faith in the process. Allow the ego to go and the energy to flow as it should. Avoid hurrying or pushing the travel.

9. Seek Advice:

Think about getting advice from a spiritual teacher or guru who has expertise with Kundalini awakening. They may provide useful insights, support, and a safe haven for your journey.

10. Be Prepared for Change:

Awakening the Kundalini is a fundamental metamorphosis that may result in powerful sensations and insights. Expect changes in your perspective, emotions, and awareness. Approach the process with an open heart and an open mind to change.

The Kundalini path for spiritual enlightenment is a very

personal and intense experience. It is a route to self-realization, inner enlightenment, and a closer relationship with the divine. Approach this trip with regard, patience, and a genuine desire to discover the infinite possibilities of your own awareness.

4. Balancing And Directing Kundalini Energy:

Kundalini energy, also known as the coiled snake at the base of the spine, has enormous transforming power. However, in order to successfully harness this great energy for spiritual progress and self-realization, it must be balanced and directed. Balancing and directing Kundalini energy is a delicate and deliberate discipline that involves awareness, patience, and competence. Here's how you can get started on your life-changing journey:

1. Grounding Techniques:

It is critical to have a solid grounding practice before trying to raise or direct Kundalini energy. Grounding helps to keep energy flowing smoothly and prevents it from becoming uncontrollable or overpowering. Practices like strolling in nature, gardening, or envisioning roots growing from your body into the Earth may help.

2. Awareness of the Chakras:

Become acquainted with the chakra system. Understanding the seven primary chakras and their characteristics is critical to maintaining a balanced flow of Kundalini energy. Meditate on each chakra on a regular basis to activate and balance their energy.

3. Kundalini Yoga:

Kundalini yoga is a particular practice for awakening, balancing, and directing Kundalini energy. To assist the flow of energy, it involves precise postures, breathwork, and meditation practices. Regular Kundalini yoga sessions may be quite useful.

4. Meditation:

Meditation is a very effective strategy for channeling Kundalini energy. Concentrate on the base of the spine and imagine a coiled snake during meditation. As your meditation practice progresses, you may direct the energy upwards via each chakra, harmonizing and purifying it as it ascends.

5. Pranayama (breath control):

Pranayama practices are very important in balancing and directing Kundalini energy. Sushumna breath, Kapalabhati, and alternate nostril breathing are all techniques that may assist move energy down the central channel. Begin with simple breathwork and work your way up as your practice grows.

6. Mantras and Sounds:

Sound vibrations are very effective instruments for dealing with Kundalini energy. Chanting certain mantras or listening to sound frequencies that resonate with the chakras may assist to guide and balance the energy.

7. Visualization:

Imagining the Kundalini energy path is a useful practice. Consider the snake uncoiling and ascending through each chakra, providing cleansing, balance, and increased consciousness at each level.

8. Energy Healing:

Participate in energy healing activities such as Reiki or Qi Gong. These treatments may aid in the removal of obstructions and the smooth flow of Kundalini energy.

9. Seek Advice:

Kundalini energy awakening and direction may be a significant and sometimes difficult journey. Seek the advice of a knowledgeable instructor or mentor who is familiar with Kundalini techniques. They can provide insights, support, and a secure space for your inquiry.

10. Accept Surrender:

Awakening the Kundalini is a path of self-discovery and change. Accept surrender and let rid of your ego. Allow the energy to flow spontaneously and trust the process. Avoid imposing or dominating your experience.

Kundalini energy is a very spiritual undertaking that must be balanced and directed. It's a route to self-realization, inner enlightenment, and a deeper relationship with the divine. Approach this trip with regard, patience, and a strong desire to realize your own consciousness's limitless potential.

CHAPTER 3: DEVELOPING PSYCHIC ABILITIES

1. Clairvoyance And Intuition

Defining Clairvoyance:

Clairvoyance is a rare skill that overcomes the constraints of our ordinary senses in the domain of extrasensory perception and psychic phenomena. The word "clairvoyance" derives from French, where "clair" means "clear" and "voyance" means "vision." Clairvoyance is the psychic skill or intuitive power to receive knowledge about people, locations, events, or things via extrasensory methods, often known as "clear seeing."

Clairvoyance extends beyond our normal sensory sense. It entails receiving mental pictures, symbols, or visions in the mind's eye without relying on the traditional five senses. These intuitive perceptions might arise spontaneously or be actively called via concentrated meditation or effort.

Clairvoyant individuals may experience these intuitive impressions as vivid mental snapshots, frequently filled with symbolic or metaphorical connotations. It's similar to having access to a secret domain of knowledge while transcending time and space boundaries.

Clairvoyance is just one aspect of a larger range of psychic skills. It may appear in a variety of ways, including:

1. Precognition: the capacity to predict future occurrences or gain insight into upcoming circumstances.

2. Retrocognition: The ability to recall facts or occurrences from the past.

3. Remote Viewing: The ability to observe or describe a distant or hidden target, which is often used in remote viewing investigations.

4. Aura Reading: The ability to sense and comprehend the energy fields or auras that surround people or things.

Clairvoyance is a kind of intuitive perception that is integrally linked to intuition. It opens the door to a greater understanding of the unseen components of reality and the mysteries of the cosmos. Those endowed with clairvoyant powers often have an increased feeling of inner knowing and may act as mediators between the physical and spiritual planes.

Developing Intuition for Success:

Intuition is a powerful force that may lead us to success in a variety of areas of our lives, from personal choices to professional activities. Developing your intuition, especially clairvoyant talents, may provide you with a competitive advantage. Here are some exercises to help you improve your clairvoyant abilities and tap into your intuitive potential for success:

1. Clarity Meditation:

Meditation is essential for strengthening your intuition. Make time for regular meditation to improve your clairvoyant talents. Concentrate on quieting your thoughts, concentrating your energies, and allowing yourself to be receptive to intuitive insights. Visualize your mind's eye opening while you meditate, enabling clear and intuitive images to flow.

2. Daily Imaginative Journal:

Begin keeping an intuitive notebook in which you write your hunches, gut emotions, and any clairvoyant experiences you have. Reflect on your submissions to see trends and improve your intuition over time. This technique teaches you to trust your instincts and interpret them correctly.

3. Visual Exercise:

Exercises that improve your visual imagination may help you increase your clairvoyance. Close your eyes and imagine other scenarios, people, or items. These mental pictures will get clearer and more detailed as you practice, strengthening your clairvoyant powers.

4. Symbol Interpretation

Experience dealing with symbols. Request that your intuition present you with a symbol or picture that contains a message. These symbols may appear to you during meditation or in ordinary settings. To get insights, trust your intuition and understand the symbols.

5. Dream Interpretation:

Be aware of your dreams and maintain a dream diary. Dreams are a rich source of clairvoyant information. Look for repeating themes, symbols, or messages in your dreams. This may be a very effective technique to improve your intuitive talents.

6. Crystal gazing:

As a focus point for your clairvoyant exercise, use a crystal ball, scrying mirror, or any reflecting surface. With an open and calm mind, look at the surface. Allow pictures and sensations to emerge before you interpret what you see.

7. Reading Object:

Hold an item, like as jewelry or a picture, and concentrate on the energy it contains. Allow your psychic skills to disclose information about the object's history, owner, or importance. This activity might help you build your intuitive connection with items over time.

8. Remote Viewing:

Experience remote seeing by trying to "see" or describe a distant or concealed target. This activity may help you hone your clairvoyant abilities and broaden your capacity to acquire information outside of your immediate surroundings.

9. Believe Your First Impressions:

Pay heed to your initial impressions and gut sentiments in everyday life. These first responses are often intuitive insights. Trust them and act on their advice while making choices, both personally and professionally.

10. Request Feedback:

Share your intuitive insights and experiences with a trusted friend or mentor who is familiar with clairvoyance or intuition. They may provide criticism and suggestions to help you improve your skills.

It takes time and determination to develop intuition and clairvoyant abilities. Your intuitive talents will increase as you practice these exercises and stay patient, giving you with a great tool for making effective decisions and attaining your objectives.

2. Telepathy And Telekinesis

Harnessing the Power of Telepathy

One of the most interesting and puzzling phenomena in parapsychology and metaphysics is telepathy. It is often defined as the capacity to send ideas, sensations, or information from one person's mind to another without using any recognized senses. Using telepathy allows for meaningful relationships and communication that go beyond the constraints of regular language. We will look at the notion of telepathy and how to develop and use this unique gift.

How to Understand Telepathy:

Telepathy is often classified into two types:

1. In this form, one person (the transmitter) projects ideas, feelings, or pictures to another person (the receiver). This technique is generally unintentional and spontaneous, but it may also be consciously created via practice.

2. Receiver-to-Sender Telepathy: This entails the receiver picking up on the sender's thoughts or feelings without any verbal or physical indications. The receiver seems to tune into the sender's mental frequency.

Consider the following methods to harness the power of telepathy:

1. Mindfulness and meditation:

Meditation is a critical exercise for enhancing psychic powers. It assists in clearing your thoughts and tuning into your intuitive senses. Regular meditation sessions might help you improve your telepathic abilities.

2. Visualization:

In your thoughts, visualize basic pictures, symbols, or scenes. Begin with basic shapes and work your way up to more complex images. This exercises your mind's ability to transmit and receive mental pictures.

3. Developing Empathy:

Empathy is an important aspect of telepathy. Develop your empathetic talents to better comprehend the feelings and ideas of others. Practice sensing other people's emotions and being more aware of their inner moods.

4. Create a Connection:

In order to practice telepathy with a partner, both people must be receptive to the experience. Select a quiet, comfortable location and sit facing each other. The transmitter should concentrate on delivering a basic concept or picture, and the recipient should be open, recording any impressions that arise.

5. Note and Reflect:

After a telepathic practice, both the transmitter and recipient should separately document their experiences. Compare notes and evaluate the transmission's correctness. This feedback loop is critical for honing your telepathic abilities.

6. Believe in Your Intuition:

Have faith in your psychic talents. Trust your intuition and your first impressions. Doubt may obstruct psychic communication.

7. Regular practice:

Telepathy is a talent that may be honed with practice. Regular practice with a partner or in a group environment may help you improve your skills.

8. Improve your telekinesis:

Telekinesis is the capacity to move or affect things using just one's thoughts. Developing telekinesis often coincides with developing telepathy. Concentrate on little, lightweight items and move them with your mind.

9. Seek Advice:

Think about receiving advice from experienced telepaths or psychics. They may provide you with insights, tactics, and mentoring to help you improve your telepathic talents.

10. Ethical Points to Consider

When participating in telepathic communication, always respect the other person's privacy and permission. Use telepathy for good, such as healing, comprehension, and connection.

Understanding and using the ability of telepathy is a voyage of self-discovery and intimate connection. As you hone these talents, you'll be able to communicate in ways other than words, broadening your knowledge of the interrelated nature of consciousness.

3. The Art Of Telekinesis:

Telekinesis, sometimes known as psychokinesis, is a fascinating and enigmatic psychic talent that includes the capacity to affect or move things with the mind's energy, rather than via traditional physical engagement. Many people have been captivated by the skill of telekinesis, which provides a look into the limitless potential of the human mind. While telekinetic phenomena is often depicted in science fiction and popular culture, people have reported experiencing them, and others have committed time and effort to developing this unusual skill.

To practice telekinesis, you must comprehend energy, intention, and attention. Here are some important stages for individuals interested in learning about telekinesis:

1. Improve Your Energy Awareness:

Before you may practice telekinesis, you must first become aware of your own energy. Practice meditation and energy work activities to increase your awareness of the subtle energy that flows inside and around you. Recognize that this energy connects everything in the cosmos, and that telekinesis is about tapping into and manipulating it.

2. Select an Object

For practice, use a lightweight, tiny item. A piece of paper, a feather, or a tiny, light item that may be readily moved without physical touch is a popular option.

3. Create the Ideal Environment

For your telekinesis practice, choose a quiet, peaceful, and concentrated atmosphere. Keep distractions to a minimum and maintain mental and emotional clarity.

4. Relax and Center:

Begin your practice by relaxing and focusing your thoughts. Meditation practices may help you quiet your thoughts and emotions. Deep, regulated breathing aids in mind clearing and goal concentration.

5. Visualize and Concentrate:

Imagine a link between yourself and the thing. Consider an energy conduit extending from your thoughts to the item. Concentrate on moving the thing and picture it occurring. Send energy to the thing using your thoughts.

6. Be Patient:

Telekinesis may not occur immediately and may proceed gradually. Be patient with yourself and keep practicing on a daily basis. It is fairly uncommon for results to take awhile to appear.

7. Keep Track of Your Experiences:

Write down your telekinesis practice sessions in a diary. Keep track of your ideas, emotions, and any changes to the item. You may examine your progress over time to uncover trends or improvements.

8. Seek Advice:

If you're serious about learning telekinesis, try consulting with a telekinesis practitioner or a psychic. They may provide ideas, approaches, and guidance to help you improve your skills.

Practical Applications of Telepathy and Telekinesis:

Telepathy and telekinesis, which are sometimes regarded as paranormal talents, have the potential for practical applications in a variety of areas of life. While developing these skills may be a personal and spiritual journey, they can also have practical uses, such as:

1. Healing and Energy Work:

Using telepathy, you may send healing energy, kind thoughts, and emotional support to anyone in need. Telepathic communication is often used by energy workers to analyze and rectify imbalances in the energy field.

2. Improved Communication:

Telepathic communication may let people communicate with one other despite linguistic and physical boundaries. It may be useful in instances when spoken or written communication is difficult, such as during an emergency or with those who have communication problems.

3. Solving Problems and Making Decisions:

Telepathy may help people solve problems and make decisions by allowing them to communicate ideas, thoughts, and information naturally. This may result in more innovative and collaborative solutions.

4. Personal Development and Self-Discovery:

Developing telepathic and telekinetic powers may be a very beneficial tool for self-discovery and personal improvement. These talents may assist people in accessing their inherent knowledge, intuition, and potential.

5. Research and Science:

Exploring telepathy and telekinesis may help scientists comprehend and investigate human awareness and mental power. Parapsychologists and consciousness researchers are interested in these occurrences.

6. Creative Expression:

Telekinesis may be used to express oneself artistically. Some artists utilize their telekinetic skills to produce unusual works of art by manipulating items to create visual representations of their ideas and feelings.

While the practical uses of telepathy and telekinesis are theoretical and not commonly acknowledged by mainstream science, exploring these skills may be an enthralling voyage of self-discovery and a method of broadening one's understanding of the mind and consciousness.

4. Astral Projection And Remote Viewing:

Out-of-Body Experiences:

Out-of-body experiences (OBEs) are extraordinary and sometimes transforming events in which a person's consciousness seems to detach from their physical body, enabling them to observe and explore the world from a vantage point outside of themselves. These experiences have been described throughout cultures and throughout history, varying in intensity and regularity. OBEs provide a rare peek into the possibilities of human consciousness and the nature of our existence outside of the physical body.

Principles of Out-of-Body Experiences:

1. Autoscopic Perception: During an OBE, people often describe seeing their own physical body from outside of it. They may report hovering above their body, gazing down on it, or watching it from a different angle.

2. Increased Sensory Awareness: OBEs often entail an increased sense of the surroundings. People who have gone out of body have experienced strong visual, aural, and sometimes touch experiences.

3. Astral go: During certain OBEs, people report to go beyond their immediate surroundings. They may explore their own houses, change rooms, or go to faraway locales. These travels are sometimes referred to as "astral travel."

4. Variability: OBEs may occur spontaneously or as a result of techniques such as meditation, lucid dreaming, or near-death experiences. They might be pleasant, neutral, or disturbing, and can last from a few seconds to many hours.

Exploring the Origins of OBEs:

The nature and interpretation of OBEs has piqued the curiosity of academics, academicians, and others interested in the mind-body link. Some of the most prevalent viewpoints and interpretations of OBEs are as follows:

1. Spiritual and metaphysical: Many people believe that OBEs are proof of the existence of a distinct, non-physical part of human awareness. These encounters are often linked to spiritual or philosophical views, implying that awareness may exist independently of the body.

2. Psychologically, OBEs may be seen as a kind of dissociation, in which the mind briefly separates from the body as a coping technique or reaction to stress, trauma, or other conditions.

3. Neuroscientists and researchers have investigated the neurological foundation of OBEs. Some speculate that these experiences are the consequence of changes in brain function, such as changes in the temporoparietal junction, which

is involved in the integration of sensory and self-related information.

4. Parapsychologists investigate OBEs as a kind of extrasensory perception (ESP). They believe that during OBEs, people collect information from their environment using unconventional methods such as remote vision.

Implications and Practical Applications:

OBEs have piqued the curiosity of researchers in a variety of domains, including psychology, neurology, and parapsychology. They have led to the investigation of the following topics:

1. notion Consciousness: OBEs call into question our notion of consciousness and its connection to the physical body. They raise issues regarding the nature of self-awareness and whether consciousness can exist independently of the brain.

2. Coping with Trauma: Some therapy treatments use OBEs to help people cope with painful situations. Viewing a distressing incident from an outside viewpoint during an OBE may help with the emotional processing involved with it.

3. OBEs serve as a focal point for parapsychological inquiries into psychic and extrasensory phenomena. These experiences are seen as proof of the presence of non-physical awareness.

4. OBEs have contributed to debates on the potential of life after death, since those who have near-death experiences may describe OBEs during these episodes. These encounters have prompted inquiry regarding the nature of existence beyond this lif

Out-of-body experiences continue to pique people's interest, spark discussion, and hold their curiosity. They continue to capture the human imagination and challenge our understanding of the borders of consciousness and the physical universe, whether considered as spiritual, psychological, or neurological occurrences.

Remote Viewing: Seeing Beyond the Physical

Remote viewing is a unique and sometimes contentious psychic phenomena in which people use extrasensory perception (ESP) to get knowledge about a distant or invisible target, place, or event. This technique extends beyond the limits of normal sensory awareness, enabling people to perceive and describe persons, places, and things to which they do not have direct access. Remote viewing has gained popularity due to its possible uses in sectors such as intelligence, research, and the discovery of the mind's capacities.

Principles of Remote Viewing

1. Non-Local Perception: The capacity to receive information about a subject that is physically distant or concealed from the observer is referred to as remote seeing. It extends beyond time and space restrictions, enabling humans to access information outside of their current sensory perspective.

2. Structured Protocol: A structured protocol or approach is often used in remote watching. A monitor or facilitator may be used to supply the viewer with minimum information on the goal, ensuring that the spectator stays unaware of the facts. The spectator then describes the target using their intuitive talents.

3. Sketches and Descriptions: Typically, remote viewers provide sketches, drawings, or textual descriptions of the objective. Details regarding the target's look, location, and other pertinent features may be included in these portrayals.

4. Training and Practice: Remote seeing is a talent that can be polished and improved with training and practice. Those who are interested in this phenomena often get training to increase their distant vision skills.

Remote Viewing Practical Applications:

Remote viewing has piqued the curiosity of scientists, intelligence agencies, and people who want to learn more about the possibilities of human awareness. The following are some practical uses and consequences of remote viewing:

1. Intelligence and Espionage: Intelligence organizations have examined and used remote viewing for its potential in acquiring information about distant or concealed targets. Some argue that remote seeing has been used in intelligence operations.

2. Remote viewing has been utilized to aid archaeologists and explorers in discovering hidden or lost historical sites and relics. It offers an unusual method for discovering hidden or inaccessible gems.

3. Health and therapeutic: Some practitioners are investigating the use of remote viewing for diagnostic and therapeutic reasons. They think that remote viewing may reveal insights into a person's physical or mental condition and aid in the identification of possible problems.

4. Personal Growth and Exploration: For those interested in the capacities of the mind, remote viewing may be used for personal growth and self-discovery. It enables individuals to push the frontiers of awareness and get a better grasp of human potential.

5. Scientists and researchers exploring consciousness and the boundaries of human perception are interested in remote watching. It raises concerns about the nature of reality and the possibility of non-local awareness.

6. Artistic and artistic Expression: Remote viewing is used by certain artists as a source of inspiration for their artistic work.

Experiences with remote viewing may result in unique creative expressions and perceptions of the world.

Remote viewing is still a topic of discussion and inquiry. While it has its detractors, supporters regard remote viewing as a window into the untapped potential of human mind and its capacity to access information beyond physical and sensory boundaries.

Using Astral Projection and Remote Viewing for Success

Astral projection and remote seeing are distinct psychic methods that may be used to achieve personal and professional goals. These skills enable people to get access to information, ideas, and viewpoints that are outside the scope of conventional perception. Here's how you can utilize astral projection and remote vision to your advantage:

1. Improved Decision-Making:

When making important judgments, use astral projection and remote vision to acquire a larger perspective. You may get insights that are not attainable via conventional methods by projecting your awareness to distant areas or obtaining information remotely. This is especially beneficial in business, where educated judgments are often the key to success.

2. Problem-Solving:

Use astral projection and remote vision to seek potential answers to complicated issues or obstacles. Your enlarged awareness might disclose hidden facets of the problem as well as novel solutions. This innovative problem-solving ability may help you stand out in your professional activities.

3. Obtaining Information:

In a professional context, you may use remote viewing to get access to data, insights, or specifics about your job. This talent may be a game changer in your job, whether it's learning about a competition, analyzing market trends, or unearthing useful information.

4. Strategic Planning

Strategic planning may benefit from astral projection and remote sight. You may foresee obstacles, appraise possibilities, and develop more educated and strong long-term plans by projecting your mind into the future or various locales.

5. Better Communication:

By employing astral projection and remote seeing to gain insight into the viewpoints and needs of others, you may improve your interpersonal skills and communication. This knowledge may help you build stronger connections with colleagues, customers, and partners, which can help you succeed professionally.

6. Increased Creativity:

Astral projection and distant viewing may help you be more creative and innovative. Exploring various habitats and dimensions allows you to get fresh experiences and ideas that may lead to breakthroughs in your profession.

7. Reduced Stress:

Astral projection and remote viewing may help you escape the stress and obligations of your working life. Regularly using these approaches may assist you in relaxing, recharging, and gaining a new perspective, allowing you to face issues with better clarity and serenity.

8. Self-Exploration:

Astral projection may be used for introspection and self-discovery. Understanding your own skills, limitations, and ambitions will assist you in setting meaningful goals and aligning your professional pursuits with your genuine self.

9. Ethical Points to Consider

While astral projection and distant seeing may provide great insights and benefits, they must be used ethically and responsibly. Respect privacy and consent, and don't use these methods for anything harmful or invasive.

10. Continuous Improvement:

Practice astral projection and remote vision on a regular basis to refine your talents and extend your potential. Seek advice from experienced practitioners or mentors who can provide useful insights and help you progress in these areas.

Astral projection and remote seeing provide a unique road to success by allowing you to delve into the depths of human consciousness and increase your understanding of the world. These qualities, when employed with integrity and purpose, may become strong instruments in accomplishing your personal and professional objectives.

CHAPTER 4: ACHIEVING SUCCESS THROUGH THIRD EYE ESP

1. Personal Transformation

Personal transformation is a profound and often lifelong journey of self-discovery and self-realization. It involves the process of evolving, growing, and becoming the best version of oneself. Self-discovery and self-realization are central components of this transformative journey, allowing individuals to uncover their true nature, purpose, and potential.

Self-Discovery and Self-Realization

Self-discovery is the process of exploring and understanding the various facets of your identity, including your thoughts, emotions, beliefs, values, strengths, weaknesses, and aspirations. It involves peeling away the layers that have been shaped by external influences, societal expectations, and past experiences. The journey of self-discovery typically includes:

1. Reflection: Taking time for self-reflection is a crucial step in self-discovery. It involves introspection, meditation, and journaling to explore your thoughts, emotions, and experiences. It allows you to become more aware of your inner world.

2. Exploration: Embrace new experiences, challenges, and adventures. By stepping outside your comfort zone, you gain new insights and perspectives on yourself and the world around you.

3. Seeking Feedback: Engage in open and honest conversations with trusted friends, mentors, or therapists who can provide valuable feedback and insights about your qualities, behaviors, and impact on others.

4. Uncovering Passions: Discover your passions and interests by experimenting with various activities and hobbies. Your passions can provide a clear sense of purpose and fulfillment.

5. Challenging Beliefs: Question your beliefs and assumptions. Consider where they originated and whether they align with your authentic self. Let go of beliefs that no longer serve you.

Self-Realization: Embracing Authenticity and Purpose

Self-realization is the culmination of self-discovery and is marked by the recognition and acceptance of your true, authentic self. It involves aligning your life with your core values, passions, and purpose. The journey of self-realization includes:

1. Authentic Living: Live in alignment with your authentic self. Make choices and decisions that resonate with your core values, rather than conforming to external expectations.

2. Passion Pursuit: Act on your passions and purpose. This often involves setting and pursuing meaningful goals that reflect your true desires and talents.

3. Empowerment: Develop a strong sense of self-worth and self-empowerment. This includes setting boundaries, asserting yourself, and making choices that serve your highest good.

4. Emotional Intelligence: Enhance your emotional intelligence by understanding and managing your emotions. This helps you build healthier relationships and navigate life's challenges with greater resilience.

5. Contribution: Consider how you can make a positive impact on others and the world. Self-realization often leads to a desire to contribute to the greater good.

6. Continued Growth: Self-realization is an ongoing process. Embrace a mindset of continuous growth and learning, and remain open to new possibilities and experiences.

Integration: The Intersection of Self-Discovery and Self-Realization

Self-discovery and self-realization are intertwined processes that continuously inform one another. Self-discovery provides the foundation for self-realization by uncovering the elements that make you unique. Self-realization, in turn, guides your choices, actions, and decisions, helping you live a more authentic, purpose-driven life.

The journey of personal transformation is a profound and often challenging endeavor. It requires courage, self-compassion, and a willingness to confront and release old patterns and limitations. However, the rewards are immense—a deeper understanding of oneself, a life aligned with purpose, and the potential for positive impact on the world.

Overcoming Limiting Beliefs and Manifesting Your Desires

Overcoming limiting beliefs and manifesting your desires are interconnected processes that empower you to create a life aligned with your true aspirations and potential. By addressing the beliefs that hold you back and using the power of intention, you can shape your reality and achieve your goals.

Overcoming Limiting Beliefs:

Limiting beliefs are self-imposed mental barriers that restrict your growth, potential, and happiness. To overcome them, you must recognize, challenge, and transform these beliefs. Here's how:

1. Awareness: Begin by becoming aware of your limiting beliefs. Pay attention to the thoughts and self-talk that create doubt or fear. Journaling can be a helpful tool to identify recurring patterns.

2. Challenge: Question the validity of your limiting beliefs. Ask yourself why you hold these beliefs and whether they are based on facts or assumptions. Challenge their accuracy and relevance to your current circumstances.

3. Reframe: Replace limiting beliefs with empowering and positive beliefs. For example, if you believe "I'm not good enough," reframe it to "I am constantly improving and growing." Develop affirmations and mantras that reinforce your new beliefs.

4. Visualization: Use visualization techniques to imagine yourself free from limiting beliefs and achieving your goals. Visualizing success can rewire your subconscious mind and boost your confidence.

5. Seek Support: Discuss your limiting beliefs with a therapist, coach, or trusted friend who can provide guidance, perspective, and encouragement. Their support can be invaluable in your transformation.

6. Take Action: Challenge your limiting beliefs by taking small steps toward your goals. Action is a powerful antidote to doubt. Celebrate your successes and acknowledge your progress.

Manifesting Your Desires:

Once you've addressed limiting beliefs, you can turn your focus to manifesting your desires and creating the life you want. Here's how to get started:

1. Clarify Your Desires: Be specific about what you want to manifest. Write down your goals, making them clear and measurable. Clarity is essential for the manifestation process.

2. Set Intentions: Set clear and positive intentions for what you want to manifest. These intentions should be aligned with your values and resonate with your authentic self.

3. Visualization: Use the power of visualization to see yourself already in possession of what you desire. Create a mental image of your desired outcome, feeling the emotions associated with success.

4. Affirmations: Affirmations can reinforce your intentions and help you stay focused on your goals. Repeatedly recite affirmations that affirm your belief in the possibility of your desires becoming a reality.

5. Action Steps: Take concrete and consistent actions toward your goals. Manifestation is not about wishful thinking alone; it involves actively working to bring your desires into reality.

6. Gratitude: Practice gratitude for what you already have and the progress you've made. This positive energy can attract more of what you desire into your life.

7. Release and Trust: Release attachment to the outcome and trust in the process. Trust that the universe is working in your favor and that your desires are on their way to manifestation.

8. Patience and Persistence: Manifestation may not happen overnight. Be patient and persistent. Keep your focus on your desires, and continue taking action.

9. Self-Belief: Believe in your own power to manifest your desires. Self-confidence and a strong belief in your abilities are key components of successful manifestation.

10. Mindfulness: Practice mindfulness to stay present and open to opportunities and synchronicities that can lead you toward your desires.

Overcoming limiting beliefs and manifesting your desires is a transformative journey that empowers you to create the life you envision. It requires self-awareness, action, and a positive mindset. With persistence and belief in your potential, you can turn your dreams into reality.

2. Relationships And Communication

Improving Interpersonal Relationships

Effective communication is at the heart of healthy, fulfilling interpersonal relationships. Whether with family, friends, colleagues, or romantic partners, the quality of your communication can significantly impact the strength and satisfaction of these connections. Here are key strategies for improving your interpersonal relationships through enhanced communication:

1. Active Listening:

Listening is a cornerstone of effective communication. Practice active listening by giving your full attention to the speaker, maintaining eye contact, and demonstrating interest in what they are saying. Reflect back what you've heard to ensure understanding. Active listening fosters empathy and connection.

2. Empathy:

Empathy is the ability to understand and share the feelings of another person. It's a crucial component of positive relationships. Cultivate empathy by putting yourself in the other person's shoes, acknowledging their emotions, and offering support and validation.

3. Nonverbal Communication:

Pay attention to your nonverbal cues, such as body language, facial expressions, and tone of voice. Ensure that your nonverbal communication aligns with your spoken words. This consistency enhances the clarity and effectiveness of your messages.

4. Open and Honest Communication:

Foster trust and transparency by communicating openly and honestly. Be willing to share your thoughts and feelings and encourage others to do the same. This level of vulnerability can deepen your relationships and resolve conflicts more effectively.

5. Conflict Resolution:

Conflict is a natural part of any relationship. Approach conflicts as opportunities for growth and understanding. Use "I" statements to express your feelings and needs, and actively seek solutions that meet both parties' interests.

6. Boundaries:

Establish and respect personal boundaries in your relationships. Boundaries define what is acceptable and comfortable for you, and communicating them to others is essential for maintaining healthy connections.

7. Appreciation and Gratitude:

Express appreciation and gratitude regularly. Let the people in your life know that you value and appreciate them. Small acts of kindness, compliments, and expressions of gratitude can strengthen your relationships.

8. Avoid Assumptions:

Avoid making assumptions about others' thoughts, feelings, or intentions. Instead, ask for clarification and seek to understand their perspective. This practice can prevent misunderstandings and unnecessary conflicts.

9. Effective Feedback:

When providing feedback or constructive criticism, be specific and focus on the behavior or issue rather than making it personal. Offer feedback with the intention of helping the other person grow and improve.

10. Quality Time:

Devote quality time to your relationships. Set aside distractions and engage in activities or conversations that nurture your connection. These moments of focused attention can deepen your bond.

11. Learn and Adapt:

Recognize that people communicate differently and have unique preferences and needs. Be open to learning about the communication style and needs of those you care about and adapt your approach accordingly.

12. Self-Awareness:

Enhance your self-awareness by reflecting on your own communication style, strengths, and weaknesses. Identify areas where you can improve and work on your self-expression, emotional regulation, and empathy.

13. Seek Professional Help:

If you encounter persistent challenges in your relationships, consider seeking the guidance of a therapist or counselor. They can provide valuable insights and strategies to help you navigate complex issues and strengthen your connections.

Improving interpersonal relationships through effective communication is an ongoing process that requires practice and self-reflection. By prioritizing these strategies, you can create more fulfilling and harmonious connections with the people in your life.

Effective Communication through ESP and Building Empathy and Understanding

Effective communication is not limited to verbal and nonverbal cues; it extends to the realm of extrasensory perception (ESP), which can foster deeper empathy and understanding in your relationships. Here's how to utilize ESP to enhance your communication and build empathy:

1. Heighten Your Awareness:

Develop your extrasensory perception by honing your intuitive abilities. Start by paying close attention to your gut feelings, hunches, and intuitive insights. The more you acknowledge and trust these sensations, the stronger your ESP becomes.

2. Meditation and Mindfulness:

Practice meditation and mindfulness to clear your mind of clutter and distractions. These techniques can help you access and interpret subtle intuitive signals more effectively.

3. Empathetic Connection:

Use your ESP to tune into the emotions and energy of others. This can enhance your ability to understand their feelings, needs, and concerns on a deeper level. Simply focus your attention on the individual and allow your intuition to guide you.

4. Visualization and Remote Viewing:

Use visualization techniques to connect with the experiences and perspectives of others. Imagine stepping into their shoes and seeing the world through their eyes. This can foster empathy and create a stronger connection in your communication.

5. Telepathy for Deeper Understanding:

Practice telepathy as a means of transmitting and receiving thoughts, emotions, and intentions. By engaging in telepathic communication, you can gain insight into the unspoken thoughts and feelings of others, leading to greater understanding.

6. Trust Your Intuition:

Build trust in your intuitive abilities. As you develop your ESP, believe in the accuracy and relevance of the insights you receive. Self-doubt can interfere with effective communication through ESP.

7. Practice Active Listening:

Combine ESP with active listening to create a deeper connection with others. Not only should you listen to the words being spoken, but also pay attention to the intuitive impressions and emotions that you pick up on during the conversation.

8. Mind-Heart Alignment:

Align your mind and heart when using ESP for communication. Your heart's intuition often provides valuable insights into emotions and empathy. Trust your heart's guidance, as it can enhance your ability to understand others.

9. Seek Feedback:

Discuss your intuitive impressions with others and seek their feedback. This open communication can confirm or clarify your intuitive insights and deepen your understanding of the people in your life.

10. Ethical Considerations:

Use your ESP for communication ethically and with the utmost respect for the privacy and consent of others. ESP should be a tool for enhancing understanding and empathy, not for intrusion or manipulation.

11. Mutual Growth:

Engage in conversations and connections that promote mutual growth. By using your ESP for communication, you can facilitate deeper and more meaningful exchanges that contribute to personal and relational development.

12. Self-Reflection:

Regularly reflect on your intuitive experiences and the impact they have on your relationships. Consider how your ESP-enhanced communication can lead to personal and mutual growth.

Effective communication through ESP can elevate your interactions to a new level of understanding and empathy. By combining your intuition with active listening and empathetic connections, you can foster deeper, more meaningful relationships with the people in your life.

3. Business And Career Enhancement

Using Third Eye ESP in Decision-Making

In the world of business and career development, making informed and strategic decisions is crucial for success. Leveraging your Third Eye extra-sensory perception (ESP) can provide a unique perspective and intuition that can lead to more effective decision-making. Here's how you can apply Third Eye ESP in your professional life:

1. Meditation and Mindfulness:

Incorporate meditation and mindfulness practices into your daily routine. These techniques can help you clear your mind, enhance your intuition, and access the wisdom of your Third Eye. Regular meditation sessions can improve your decision-making abilities.

2. Developing Intuition:

Pay attention to your intuitive insights and hunches. These often come from the intuitive powers of your Third Eye. Cultivate trust in your intuition by documenting and reflecting on instances where it guided you to successful decisions.

3. Expanding Your Awareness:

Use your Third Eye to expand your awareness and gain a deeper understanding of complex business situations. Visualize and sense the various facets of a decision, considering not only the immediate consequences but also the long-term impact.

4. Foresight and Insight:

Utilize your Third Eye to anticipate challenges, trends, and opportunities in your industry. This foresight can help you make proactive and strategic decisions, staying ahead of the curve.

5. Problem-Solving:

When faced with a challenging problem, allow your Third Eye to guide your problem-solving process. Visualize potential solutions and let your intuition help you select the most appropriate course of action.

6. Releasing Limiting Beliefs:

Address any limiting beliefs or biases that may be clouding your judgment. Your Third Eye can assist in revealing these subconscious limitations, allowing you to make decisions that are not hindered by preconceived notions.

7. Empathetic Decision-Making:

Employ your Third Eye's intuitive powers to consider the needs and feelings of others. This empathetic approach can lead to more inclusive and ethical decision-making in your professional interactions.

8. Visualization and Goal Setting:

Use visualization techniques to set and clarify your career and business goals. Your Third Eye can assist in creating a clear mental image of your objectives and guide you toward decisions that align with these aspirations.

9. Ethical and Responsible Use:

Apply your Third Eye ESP ethically and responsibly in your professional life. Avoid using it to gain unfair advantages or manipulate outcomes. Instead, use it to promote integrity, fairness, and personal and professional growth.

10. Continuous Learning:

Continue to develop your Third Eye and intuitive abilities through education and practice. Seek guidance from experienced mentors or practitioners who can help you refine your skills and navigate complex decisions.

11. Reflection and Feedback:

Reflect on your decisions and outcomes, seeking feedback from trusted colleagues or mentors. This reflective process can help you refine your decision-making abilities and adapt for the future.

12. Balancing Logic and Intuition:

Integrate your Third Eye's intuition with logical reasoning in your decision-making process. Striking a balance between your intuitive insights and rational analysis can lead to well-rounded and effective decisions.

By incorporating Third Eye ESP into your business and career decision-making, you can tap into a deeper well of intuition and awareness. This enhanced perspective can lead to more strategic, ethical, and successful choices in your professional life.

Career Advancement and Problem-Solving

Advancing in your career often involves overcoming challenges and making strategic decisions. Leveraging your skills and abilities for problem-solving can significantly impact your professional growth. Here's how to apply your problem-solving skills to advance your career:

1. Analytical Thinking: Develop strong analytical skills to dissect complex issues and identify the root causes of problems. A logical, data-driven approach can lead to effective solutions in your career.

2. Strategic Planning: Create a career development plan that outlines your short-term and long-term goals. This strategy will help you stay focused and organized, allowing you to overcome obstacles and advance.

3. Decision-Making: Make well-informed decisions by considering all relevant factors. Using your intuition, guided by your Third Eye, can enhance the quality of your choices.

4. Networking: Build and maintain a professional network to gain support and insights. Networking can provide you with valuable perspectives and potential solutions to career challenges.

5. Adaptability: Be open to change and flexible in your approach to problem-solving. Adaptability is essential as you navigate a dynamic career landscape.

6. Learning and Skill Development: Continuously invest in your education and skill development. Acquiring new knowledge and capabilities can empower you to tackle complex challenges and progress in your career.

7. Resilience: Develop emotional resilience to face setbacks and failures. Resilience will enable you to bounce back from difficulties and persevere in your career journey.

8. Conflict Resolution: Hone your conflict resolution skills to address workplace issues and disagreements constructively. Effective conflict resolution can maintain positive relationships and create a more harmonious work environment.

9. Feedback Seeker: Be open to feedback and seek it actively from colleagues, mentors, and supervisors. Constructive feedback can help you identify areas for improvement and refine your problem-solving strategies.

10. Mentorship: Seek guidance and mentorship from experienced professionals in your field. Mentors can provide valuable insights, share their problem-solving expertise, and accelerate your career advancement.

Entrepreneurial Success and Innovation

Entrepreneurship is a realm where innovation and creative problem-solving are vital for success. Whether you're starting a new venture or growing an existing business, these principles can guide your entrepreneurial journey:

1. Innovation Culture: Foster a culture of innovation within your entrepreneurial team or organization. Encourage employees to think creatively and propose innovative solutions to business challenges.

2. Market Research: Prioritize market research to identify unmet needs, trends, and opportunities. Innovate by offering products or services that address these gaps.

3. Customer-Centric Approach: Place the customer at the center of your innovation process. Seek feedback and insights from your target audience to create products or services that genuinely meet their needs.

4. Risk Management: Entrepreneurship often involves calculated risks. Use your analytical skills to assess potential risks and rewards, and make informed decisions.

5. Adaptation: Embrace adaptability as an entrepreneur. The business landscape can change rapidly, and being willing to adapt and pivot in response to new challenges is key to long-term success.

6. Problem-Solving Mindset: Approach business challenges as opportunities for innovation. Use your problem-solving skills to find creative solutions that give you a competitive advantage.

7. Resource Management: Efficiently manage your resources, including finances, time, and personnel. This ensures you have the means to support your innovative ventures.

8. Networking and Collaboration: Collaborate with other entrepreneurs, professionals, and organizations to share insights, pool resources, and create innovative solutions together.

9. Entrepreneurial Resilience: Entrepreneurship can be challenging, and resilience is essential. Develop the ability to bounce back from setbacks and maintain your drive and passion for innovation.

10. Scaling and Growth: As your entrepreneurial venture succeeds, focus on scalable growth strategies. This includes expanding your market reach, diversifying product lines, and exploring new opportunities for innovation.

11. Ethical and Sustainable Innovation: Prioritize ethical and sustainable practices in your entrepreneurial endeavors. Innovations that align with ethical and environmental standards can set you apart in the market.

By combining problem-solving skills with a commitment to innovation, you can advance your career and achieve entrepreneurial success. These principles will help you navigate challenges, seize opportunities, and continue to grow and innovate in your professional journey.

4. Health And Wellness:

Holistic Healing with Third Eye ESP

Holistic healing, which considers the well-being of the mind, body, and spirit, can be enhanced with the use of your Third Eye extra-sensory perception (ESP). This spiritual and intuitive approach to wellness allows you to address health concerns from a comprehensive perspective. Here's how you can apply your

Third Eye ESP for holistic healing:

1. Mind-Body Connection:

Tap into the mind-body connection using your Third Eye. Visualize the energy flow within your body, and use your intuitive insights to identify areas of tension or imbalance. This can guide you in addressing physical and emotional issues simultaneously.

2. Stress Reduction:

Use your Third Eye to identify the sources of stress in your life. Visualize stress as a tangible force, and then release it through meditation, relaxation, and other stress-reduction techniques. Reducing stress is a fundamental step in holistic healing.

3. Energy Healing:

Direct your intuitive energy to areas of the body that require healing. Visualization and energy work can help restore balance and harmony, promoting overall well-being and alleviating physical and emotional discomfort.

4. Meditation and Mindfulness:

Incorporate meditation and mindfulness into your daily routine. These practices help you connect with your Third Eye, allowing you to access deeper insights and a sense of inner peace. A calm mind supports holistic healing.

5. Nutrition and Intuition:

Combine your intuition with your dietary choices. Use your Third

Eye to tune into the needs of your body, helping you select foods that nourish your physical and spiritual well-being. Intuitive eating can promote health and vitality.

6. Emotional Release:

Use your Third Eye to identify and release unresolved emotions and past traumas. Visualization can guide you in letting go of emotional baggage, contributing to mental and emotional healing.

7. Pain Management:

Visualize your body's energy and focus your intuitive abilities on areas of pain or discomfort. Use this heightened awareness to explore pain management techniques such as relaxation, mindfulness, or alternative therapies.

8. Chakra Balancing:

The chakra system plays a significant role in holistic healing. Use your Third Eye to assess and balance your chakras. Visualize each energy center as you work to remove blockages and enhance energy flow.

9. Self-Healing Visualization:

Visualize your body in a state of perfect health and wellness. This self-healing visualization can stimulate your body's natural healing mechanisms and promote physical well-being.

10. Holistic Practitioner Guidance:

Consult with holistic health practitioners who can support your journey. Many practitioners integrate intuitive and energy-based approaches into their healing practices.

11. Self-Care and Self-Love:

Cultivate self-care practices and self-love. Your Third Eye can guide you in identifying self-care activities that resonate with your individual needs, nurturing your overall wellness.

12. Ethical and Responsible Use:

Apply your Third Eye ESP for holistic healing ethically and with integrity. Respect the privacy and consent of others when using your intuitive abilities in healing practices.

13. Continuous Growth:

Holistic healing is an ongoing process. Embrace a mindset of continuous growth and exploration. Regularly practice and refine your Third Eye abilities to support your holistic well-being.

Stress Reduction and Emotional Balance

ESP allows you to address health and wellness from a comprehensive and spiritual perspective. By incorporating these practices into your life, you can promote balance, healing, and overall well-being.Stress Reduction and Emotional Balance

Stress can take a toll on both your physical and emotional well-being. Balancing your emotional state and reducing stress is crucial for holistic health. Here's how you can leverage your Third

Eye ESP to achieve emotional balance and reduce stress:

1. Identifying Stressors:

Use your Third Eye to identify the sources of stress in your life. Visualization can help you pinpoint specific stressors, whether they are related to work, relationships, or personal concerns.

2. Emotional Release:

Visualize stress and negative emotions as tangible energy. Use your intuitive abilities to release this energy through meditation, deep breathing, and other relaxation techniques. This process can help you achieve emotional balance.

3. Mindfulness and Meditation:

Incorporate mindfulness and meditation practices to connect with your Third Eye. These techniques can enhance your self-awareness, emotional regulation, and ability to manage stress effectively.

4. Intuitive Decision-Making:

When faced with stressful decisions, trust your intuitive insights guided by your Third Eye. This can help you make choices that align with your inner wisdom, reducing the emotional burden of uncertainty.

5. Energy Healing for Emotional Release:

Direct your intuitive energy toward emotional blockages. Visualize these blockages dissipating, allowing the flow of positive energy and emotional healing. Energy healing techniques like Reiki can be especially effective.

6. Visualization for Emotional Balance:

Visualize your emotional state as a calm, serene lake. Use your Third Eye to maintain this visualization during times of stress. This mental image can help you stay centered and emotionally balanced.

7. Chakra Balancing:

Work on balancing your chakras to promote emotional well-being. Your Third Eye can guide you in this process, ensuring that energy flows freely through your chakra system.

8. Positive Affirmations:

Create positive affirmations that reinforce emotional balance and resilience. Use these affirmations in your daily life to shift your mindset and reduce stress.

9. Journaling and Self-Reflection:

Use your Third Eye to explore your thoughts and emotions through journaling and self-reflection. This self-awareness can provide insight into the roots of stress and emotional imbalances.

10. Self-Compassion and Self-Love:

Practice self-compassion and self-love. Use your Third Eye to guide you in embracing self-care routines that nurture your emotional well-being.

11. Ethical and Responsible Use:

Apply your Third Eye ESP for emotional balance and stress reduction ethically and with integrity. Respect the privacy and consent of others when using your intuitive abilities for emotional support.

12. Support Network:

Lean on your support network when needed. Seek guidance and emotional support from trusted friends, family, or therapists to help you navigate challenging emotional periods.

Boosting Physical and Mental Health

Your Third Eye ESP can also play a role in enhancing your physical and mental health. Here are ways you can utilize your intuitive abilities for holistic health:

1. Visualization for Healing:

Visualize your body in a state of perfect health. Use your Third Eye to guide this visualization, focusing on areas that may require healing or support.

2. Energy Healing:

Engage in energy healing practices, such as Reiki, to promote physical and mental well-being. Use your intuitive insights to direct healing energy where it is needed.

3. Holistic Nutrition:

Intuitively select foods and supplements that support your physical and mental health. Your Third Eye can guide you in making choices that resonate with your body's needs.

4. Stress Reduction Techniques:

Utilize your intuitive abilities to enhance stress reduction techniques. Visualization, meditation, and mindfulness can be more effective when guided by your Third Eye.

5. Pain Management:

Use your Third Eye to focus on areas of physical discomfort. Visualization and energy work can help reduce pain and promote healing.

6. Emotional Healing:

Address emotional issues that may be affecting your mental health. Your Third Eye can guide you in understanding and releasing unresolved emotions that impact your mental well-being.

7. Self-Healing Visualization:

Visualize yourself as a whole, healthy being, mentally and physically. This self-healing visualization can stimulate your body's natural healing mechanisms.

8. Mind-Body Connection:

Explore the connection between your mental and physical health. Use your Third Eye to detect how emotional well-being affects physical health and vice versa.

9. Ethical and Responsible Use:

Apply your Third Eye ESP for physical and mental health ethically and with respect for your own privacy and well-being. Be responsible in your use of intuitive abilities.

10. Seek Professional Guidance:

Consult with healthcare professionals and mental health experts when needed. Your Third Eye can guide you in selecting the right practitioners and approaches to support your holistic health.

By integrating your Third Eye ESP into your approach to emotional balance, stress reduction, and holistic health, you can create a more comprehensive and intuitive approach to your well-being, fostering both physical and mental health.

CHAPTER 5: CHALLENGES AND ETHICAL CONSIDERATIONS

1. The Dark Side Of Esp

Extra-Sensory Perception (ESP) has a negative side even if it has the potential to reveal remarkable insights and skills. This section examines the dangers, moral dilemmas, and possible obstacles related to ESP:

Exploring the Ethical Dilemmas

The pursuit of psychic talents, such as Extra-Sensory Perception (ESP), may give rise to significant ethical dilemmas. Here, we examine a few moral conundrums relating to psychic abilities:

1. Invasion of Privacy:

Invasive Insights: Psychic people may unintentionally or purposely learn about other people's innermost feelings and thoughts. Consent and honoring one's own limits are called into doubt by this invasion.

Respecting Privacy: A basic ethical challenge is finding a balance between recognizing one's psychic skills and honoring the privacy of others.

2. Boundaries and Consent:

Informed permission: Informed permission is necessary when using psychic powers for the benefit of others, as in readings or consultations. Customers have a right to know what restrictions will be put in place and how their personal information will be used.

limits: Psychics need to be careful to set up limits with their clientele so they don't exploit or manipulate weak people.

3. Conscience Obligation:

Using Abilities Ethically: Rather of abusing their skills for manipulation or self-interest, psychics have an ethical duty to utilize their abilities for the benefit of society at large. They should provide insights, counsel, and assistance.

Halving Truth and Compassion: Psychics should make an effort to tell the truth while taking the clients' emotional health into account.

4. Credibility and Skepticism:

Preserving Credibility: Psychics that make outlandish claims might come under investigation and criticism. It is ethical to maintain credibility by providing proof or affirmation of their skills.

Respecting Skeptics: Although it's important for psychics to stand by their experiences, ethical behavior may be encouraged by listening to skeptics' opinions and having productive conversations with them.

5. Wise Decisions:

Vulnerable Individuals: Some individuals may seek the advice of psychics when they are in a vulnerable emotional condition. Rather of depending entirely on their intuitive insights, ethical psychics should make sure that their customers are making well-informed decisions.

Empowerment: An ethical strategy is to provide clients the freedom to make their own choices rather than depending only on psychic guidance.

6. Misplaced Hope:

Managing Expectations: Managing client expectations is a duty that comes with providing psychic insights. Giving a fair-minded viewpoint helps avoid relying too much on psychic readings.

Avoiding False Promises: It is unethical to guarantee cures or miraculous results in the absence of supporting data.

7. False Statements:

Avoiding Deception: Morally upright psychics should abstain from manipulative or misleading techniques like cold readings.

Transparency: Ethical behavior requires transparency on the techniques and resources used in psychic readings.

8. Stigmatization and Discrimination:

Respect and Inclusion: Psychics need to abstain from prejudice towards others who do not have similar views or life experiences. Encouraging inclusivity and respect is morally required.

9. The Moral Obligation to Advance Skill Development:

Personal Development: In order to guarantee the precision and dependability of their insights, psychic people have an ethical duty to continuously learn and hone their abilities.

10. Reliability:

Protecting Clients: A fundamental component of moral psychic practices is upholding client confidentiality. Information disclosed during readings need to be kept private unless the recipient expressly grants permission to do so.

Coping with the Challenges of Psychic Abilities

Psychic skills provide certain difficulties in addition to being entertaining and illuminating. Here are some strategies for people to overcome these difficulties:

1. Self-Understanding:

Reflecting on Experiences: Having a thorough grasp of one's psychic experiences, along with its advantages and disadvantages, may help people handle any difficulties they may run across.

2. Moral Reflections:

Ethical Framework: Provide a solid moral foundation for the use of psychic talents. This might serve as advice on how to behave in a responsible and courteous manner.

3. Considering Skepticism:

- Interacting Constructively: Have an open and productive dialogue with doubters and critics. Their viewpoints might provide insightful information and help psychic people stay grounded.

4. Self-Growth:

Emotional Resilience: To manage the possible difficulties of being a psychic, cultivate emotional resilience. Important elements include stress management, mindfulness, and self-care.

5. Boundaries and Privacy:

Clear Boundaries: Establish precise guidelines for when and how to employ psychic skills, taking other people's privacy and permission into consideration.

6. Seek Assistance:

Community: Make connections with groups of psychics or like-minded people who may provide support, understanding, and direction.

7. Constant Expansion:

Personal Development: Constantly focus on your own growth, including strengthening your psychic powers and a strong moral compass.

8. Specialist Advice:

Mentorship: Seek the advice and direction of seasoned psychics who can assist you in navigating the difficulties and moral dilemmas associated with psychic skills.

9. Transparency:

Honesty: When offering people your thoughts, be open and honest about your strengths and weaknesses. One essential element of ethical behavior is honesty.

Self-awareness, moral behavior, a dedication to personal development, and a determination to using these special powers responsibly are necessary for overcoming the problems of psychic abilities. People may more successfully traverse the complicated world of psychic talents by realizing these difficulties and engaging them with honesty.

2. Ethical Use Of Third Eye Powers:

Responsible Psychic Practices

Those who are psychic and use the Third Eye have a great obligation to behave morally and responsibly. Here, we look at how to use appropriate psychic activities to guarantee the moral application of Third Eye abilities:

1. Conscientious Assent:

Respect Boundaries: Always respect people's privacy and personal space. Before trying to access their thoughts or feelings, get their informed permission.

Educate Clients: Inform clients about the nature and limitations of Third Eye insights. Motivate them to make well-informed decisions.

2. Sincerity and Openness:

Truthful Communication: Describe your skills in an open and sincere manner. Steer clear of making inflated statements or unsubstantiated promises.

Explain the Process: Give an explanation of the psychic reading or consultation process, along with the instruments or techniques you use. Make sure your consumers know exactly what to anticipate.

3. Reliability:

Client Privacy: Make sure that any information disclosed during readings is kept private unless the recipient expressly gives permission to do so.

4. Data Security:

Comply with data protection laws and standards and take the greatest precautions when protecting any customer data and personal information.

5. Strengthening:

Support Client Decision-Making: Give clients the tools they need to decide for themselves based on the information presented. Motivate people to accept responsibility for their decisions and lives.

 Avoid Dependency: Urge clients to look for advice from a variety of sources and to avoid being too dependent on your psychic revelations.

5. Non-Discrimination:

Inclusivity: Show respect to every person, irrespective of their circumstances, background, or beliefs. Avoid prejudice, discrimination, and judgment in any form.

Cultural Sensitivity: Take note of cultural variances and make sure your psychic work is inclusive and mindful of many viewpoints.

6. Limitations:

Clarity of Ethical Boundaries: Define precise moral limits for the use of your psychic skills. Clearly state what you will and won't do or interpret.

7. Respect Personal limits:

When dealing with customers and other people, respect your personal limits. Never trespass into their private affairs without their permission.

8. Criticism and Doubt:

Talk to Skeptics: Talk to critics and skeptics in a positive way. Take into account their viewpoints and properly handle any issues.

Evidence-Based Practice: Whenever feasible, use evidence-based techniques to support the precision and potency of your psychic insights.

8. Sensible Utilization of Knowledge:

Avoid Manipulation: Refrain from controlling or manipulating others using your Third Eye abilities. Honor their decisions and freedom of choice.

Conflict of Interest: At readings or consultations, disclose any possible conflicts of interest that could compromise your impartiality and objectivity.

9. Self-Growth:

Emotional Resilience: To handle the emotional demands of psychic work, develop emotional resilience. Take care of yourself in order to preserve your own wellbeing.

10. Ongoing Education:

Ongoing Development: Make a commitment to lifelong study and growth to expand your psychic skills and uphold moral behavior.

Mentorship: Seek guidance from seasoned psychics or mentors who can assist you with challenging circumstances and advise you on moral behavior.

11. Advertising Ethics:

Honest Marketing: Make sure that all promotions and advertisements fairly depict your skills, methods, and services.

Avoid Guarantees: Refrain from providing unqualified assurances about results since they may be deceptive and immoral.

12. Appropriate Behavior with Vulnerable People:

Special Care: Exercise extra caution while interacting with those who are susceptible, such as bereaved or experiencing emotional distress. Provide assistance and direction, but take additional precautions to make sure they're safe.

13. Ethical Obligation to Society:

Social Responsibility: Be aware of your moral obligation to society. Put your Third Eye abilities to use by providing wisdom and direction to advance beneficial change and wellbeing.

In order to guarantee that the use of Third Eye abilities is advantageous to both people and society at large, responsible psychic practices that are based on ethics and integrity are crucial. By adhering to these moral guidelines, psychics may use their special powers while preserving a feeling of duty to the welfare and moral treatment of others.

Helping Others with ESP

Helping people is one of the most purposeful uses of ESP and psychic skills. Here are a few morally and responsibly acceptable methods to help people with ESP:

1. Empathy & Compassion:

Deal with others empathetically and compassionately, taking into account their worries and feelings. It is possible to establish a secure atmosphere for them to open up by being supportive and kind.

2. Conscientious Assent:

Before utilizing your ESP to assist someone, be sure they have given their informed permission. Make sure they know what kind of help you are providing and how much you will be using your skills.

3. Honoring Boundaries:

Honor individual privacy rights and limitations. If someone has given you permission to access their thoughts or feelings and is comfortable with it, then only use your ESP to probe into their mind or feelings.

4. Customer Empowerment:

Give them the freedom to decide for themselves using the information you supply. Urge them to take responsibility for their life and the routes they decide to follow.

5. Moral Counsel:

Give moral advice based on your observations, keeping the welfare of the people you're helping in mind at all times. Urge them to take actions that further the greater good and are consistent with their principles.

6. Prevent Reliance:

Encourage people to consult both conventional and psychic sources for advice. Encourage them not to rely too much on your knowledge.

7. Conscientious Disclosure:

Acknowledge the possibility of errors and the limits of your ESP. Be truthful and upright in all of your dealings.

8. Emotional Assistance:

Provide emotional assistance in addition to your psychic abilities. People who are in need often gain by having someone to listen to them and show them care.

9. Culturally Attuned:

It is important to have an open mind and show cultural sensitivity while helping people from diverse backgrounds. Honor their traditions and values.

10. Continuous Development:

Make a commitment to constant self-improvement to raise the potency and accuracy of your psychic skills. You can help others more effectively thanks to this ongoing progress.

Maintaining Personal Integrity

Retaining one's integrity is essential to using ESP responsibly. Here's how to make sure your deeds reflect your beliefs and ideals:

1. Introspection:

- Reflect on your activities on a regular basis to make sure they are consistent with your integrity and ideals.

2. Sincerity and Openness:

- Be truthful and open in all of your communications. Maintain a dedication to honesty and transparency in both your personal and professional life.

3. Making Ethical Decisions:

- Base your moral judgments on your values and moral compass. Think about how your decisions will affect other people and society.

4. Responsibility:

- Accept responsibility for your deeds and the consequences of them. If you make a mistake, own up to it and take steps to fix it.

5. courtesy toward others:

- Be mindful of and respectful of other people's privacy, boundaries, and emotions. Be nice and understanding to others.

6. Limitations:

- Establish and maintain personal limits to safeguard your health and make sure your morals aren't being compromised.

7. Don't manipulate:

- Avoid manipulating or tricking others with your psychic talents.

uphold a dedication to justice and integrity.

8. Constant Self-Development:

- Strive for ongoing development of your psychic skills as well as your character. Make an effort to be your best self.

9. Ethical Obligation to Society:

Acknowledge your moral obligation to the community. Make good use of your psychic and extrasensory perception skills to improve the lives of people and the planet.

10. Seek Assistance and Direction:

Seek mentorship and assistance from peers or mentors who share your dedication to moral behavior and honesty. Study their knowledge and experiences.

You may live a life that is consistent with your beliefs and ideals and have a significant and positive influence on the lives of people you serve by using your ESP to help others and maintaining your integrity.

3. Staying Grounded

Balancing the Spiritual and Material Worlds

Balancing the spiritual and material parts of life is one of the biggest obstacles facing those with ESP and psychic skills. Here's how to navigate these two worlds without losing your bearings:

1. Introspection:

- Reflect on yourself often to gain insight into your wants, motives, and values in both the spiritual and material spheres of life.

2. Make Your Intentions Clear:

- Clearly state your aims. Know why you are utilizing your ESP and how it relates to your life's spiritual and material facets.

3. Everyday Customs:

- Create regular routines that help you stay grounded in reality. You may maintain your feeling of balance by engaging in grounding exercises, meditation, or time spent in nature.

4. Realistic anticipations are:

- Have reasonable goals for both your spiritual and monetary aspirations. Recognize that finding a balance may involve persistence and flexibility.

5. Limitations:

- Define boundaries between your personal and professional life as a psychic. Don't allow one take precedence over the other; instead, set aside dedicated time for both.

6. Community Participation:

Engage in communal and social events to maintain a connection to the physical world. A feeling of purpose and belonging that goes beyond your psychological experiences might come from this.

7. Personal Connections:

- Develop close friendships and familial ties. You might feel anchored and reminded of the value of interpersonal relationships by these connections.

8. Support System:

- Retain a network of people who can guide and empathize with you, since they understand your experiences.

9. Ethical Behavior:

- Use a strong ethical framework while using your psychic powers, making sure that your acts are consistent with your spiritual and material values.

10. Self-Growth:

- Make self-care a priority to preserve your physical and emotional health. To remain centered, make sure you are taking good care of your body and mind.

11. Being mindful:

- Use mindfulness techniques to maintain present-moment awareness. You may enjoy both the material world and spiritual experiences more if you practice mindful awareness.

12. Consistency in Decisions:

- Take into account both the spiritual and material aspects of choices you make in life. Make decisions that demonstrate a balanced combination of these two factors.

13. Seek Advice:

Seek counsel from mentors or spiritual counselors who may provide direction on striking a balance between life's spiritual and material aspects.

14. Maintain a Journal:

- Keep a notebook in which you may jot down your ideas, observations, and experiences on the harmony between the material and spiritual realms.

15. Regular Rest Periods:

- Take frequent pauses from concentrated cerebral effort to participate in commonplace activities that foster a sense of physical connection.

16. Seek Expert Assistance:

- If you struggle to remain grounded and in balance, think about getting professional help from therapists or counselors who focus on psychological and spiritual well-being.

17. Spiritual Alignment:

Examine how you may incorporate your spiritual experiences into your day-to-day activities. This may include making spiritual activities and insights a part of your daily life.

Maintaining a balance between the material and spiritual realms calls for self-awareness, dedication, and a deliberate way of living. You may utilize your ESP and psychic skills to improve both your spiritual development and your interaction with the outside world by keeping this balance.

4. Avoiding Ego Inflation

For those with ESP and psychic powers to preserve humility and moral behavior, ego inflating must be avoided. Here's how to control your ego:

1. Introspection:

- Evaluate your aims and reasons on a regular basis. Think back on what you've done and ask yourself whether it's out of self-interest or a sincere desire to assist and develop.

2. Humility:

- Develop humility as a fundamental virtue. Keep in mind that having psychic powers does not make you better than other people; rather, it is simply one facet of who you are.

3. Conscience Obligation:

Acknowledge that it is your moral duty to use your skills for the benefit of society as a whole rather than advancing your own goals or ego.

4. Sincere Remarks:

Ask for frank feedback from peers or mentors who can support you in staying grounded and, if necessary, provide helpful criticism.

5. Continue to Have a Support System:

- Create a support system of people around you who can give you advice and hold you responsible for your actions.

6. Don't Be Grandiose:

- Refrain from making exaggerated promises about your skills or potential influence. Keep an accurate perspective of your ability.

7. Check Yourself:

- Consistently check in with yourself to make sure your choices and behaviors are not driven by a need to outdo others.

8. Continue Learning:

Be devoted to lifelong study and development. Acknowledging that there is always more to learn and comprehend might aid in avoiding ego inflate and complacency.

9. Keep Your Ground:

- Practice grounding techniques, including mindfulness and meditation, to maintain your inner connection and keep your ego from taking over.

10. Utilizing insights ethically:

- Make ethical and responsible use of your psychic insights, putting more of an emphasis on serving others than on flaunting your skills for your own glorification.

Using Mindfulness in Everyday Situations

Being mindful may help you be more present, feel less stressed, and be more aware of yourself. How to Apply Mindfulness in Your Everyday Life:

1. Morning Schedule:

- Set up a thoughtful morning ritual to start your day. This might be deep breathing exercises, meditation, or some time spent thinking about your goals for the day.

2. Conscious Eating:

- Pay attention to the flavor, texture, and aroma of your food while you consume. Stay focused and enjoy every meal.

3. Grounding Methodologies:

Employ grounding exercises to focus on the here and now, such as interacting with nature or experiencing the texture of items.

4. Practice Breathing:

To keep calm and manage stress, try deep breathing techniques. This may be very useful when handling difficult circumstances.

5. Observant Motion:

- To synchronize your body and mind, practice mindful movement techniques like yoga or tai chi.

6. Thankfulness Journal:

- Maintain a gratitude notebook where you may write down all the things you have to be grateful for. This may help you concentrate on the good.

7. Unprejudiced Awareness:

- Examine your feelings and ideas without passing judgment. Accept them as they are without placing any value judgments on them.

8. Mindful Interaction:

- Engage in mindful conversation by paying attention to what other people are saying, speaking slowly, and being completely present.

9. Cyber Detox:

- Take frequent breaks from electronic screens. Engage with the people and environment around you mindfully.

10. Evening Thought:

- Finish the day by reflecting mindfully on your experiences and deeds. You may absorb the events and be ready for a good night's sleep by doing this.

11. Stimulated Walking:

- Make mindful walking a part of your everyday schedule. As you go, be mindful of every step and your environment.

12. Art or creativity that is mindful:

- Create attentively when doing artistic endeavors like writing, painting, or music. Let your art come to you organically and without concern about the results.

13. Rectal Scan:

- To connect with your body and let go of stress, try a body scan meditation.

14. Every Day Declarations:

- Begin each day with affirmations that are consistent with your goals and beliefs. Utilize them all day to direct your behavior and attitude.

15. Breathe Consciously Throughout the Day:

- Include attentive breathing in your everyday activities. Pause for a minute and concentrate on your breathing, particularly in trying or stressful circumstances.

You may develop a feeling of present, control your ego, and improve your self-awareness by incorporating mindfulness practices into your everyday routine. You may maintain a healthy, moral connection to your psychic skills while being grounded, balanced, and mindful.

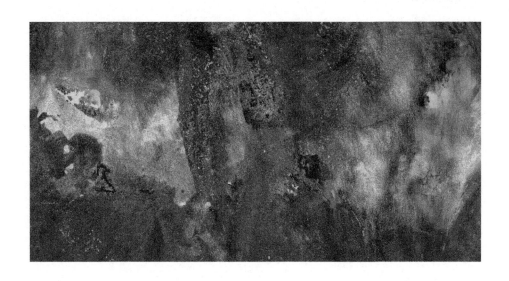

CHAPTER 6: THE JOURNEY AHEAD

1. Cultivating A Lifelong Practice

The voyage is a lifetime undertaking and a constantly changing tapestry of discovery in the Land of the Mind's Eye. It's a way of life, a dedication to raising your awareness and accepting life's mysteries rather than a goal.

Consider the third eye as a cosmic entrance that leads to the unknown. This marks the actual start of our journey. It's an expedition into self-reflection and a quest for secrets both within and outside of yourself. The spheres of intuition, insight, and inner vision are always being explored.

The Third Eye is more than just a tool; it's a spiritual extension that is a mystery that has to be solved.

A Career-Long Interest:

The Third Eye encourages us to slow down and enjoy the trip itself in our constantly connected society where quick satisfaction is the norm. It's about losing yourself in the intricate web of your own mind and the universe, not in short cuts or instant solutions.

Remind yourself that perseverance and commitment are your compass points as you develop your lifetime practice.

The Enigmatic Peak:

There are several peaks of discovery along the way of your trip. Instead, it's a journey across enormous, mysterious landscapes. Enjoy the vista when you reach the heights of knowledge, but remember that there are still many more peaks to discover.

Like the world, the Third Eye is always growing.

The Skill of Combination:

It is not intended for the Third Eye to be an isolated activity. It's about incorporating the realizations and insights into your day-to-day activities. It's about accepting your psychic abilities, living with an elevated level of consciousness, and perceiving the invisible.

Every day is a canvas, and you are the painter who uses the brushstrokes of your awakened awareness to create your reality.

The Alchemical Insider:

Your trip via the Third Eye is an alchemical process that turns the commonplace aspects of life into the remarkable knowledge that is like gold. It's about searching inside for the self-realization philosopher's stone and the elixir of enlightenment.

You'll learn the genuine essence of your spirit in the trial and testing of your life.

The Interminable Tale:

You are the main character in the epic that is your Third Eye trip. New mysteries and difficulties are revealed in every chapter, but keep in mind that the narrative never really ends. It keeps changing, evolving, and inspiring.

The threads of your Third Eye trip bind the pages of your life, and they spin with every conscious breath.

Final Thoughts:

Let these words serve as your candle in the dark, leading you through the maze-like passageways of the secrets of the Third Eye, as we come to an end to this chapter and get ready to explore the next.

The Third Eye voyage is a work of art, and you are the creator using your vision to paint the universe.

May your journey be filled with unending amazement, unbridled curiosity, and the unshakeable understanding that your Third Eye holds the secret to the universe. I hope your investigation leads you to the everlasting realization that the journey is the goal in and of itself.

Continue to be alert, to be motivated, and to travel.

Go forth, my fellow aspirant.

Honing Your Psychic Skills Over Time:

The process of developing psychic abilities is comparable to a sculptor perfecting a work of art by chiseling away at the rough stone to expose its inner beauty. Like this ageless art, your psychological journey develops and deepens with time. It is a lifetime marathon, a gradual awakening, and an ongoing process of self-discovery; it is not a race.

Revealing the Inside Masterpiece

Imagine yourself working as a consciousness-based sculptor. Every meditation is a brushstroke, and every psychological encounter is a blow to the chisel. You discover more of the masterpiece inside yourself with each interaction.

Your intuitive gifts are the masterpiece just waiting to be discovered.

A Method Extending Time:

The passage of time has no effect on the path of mastering psychic abilities. It extends into days, months, and years, beyond seconds and minutes. Time is your friend and a patient tutor who is waiting for you to realize all of your potential.

You get more in touch with the ethereal melody of existence with every passing moment.

Patience's Wisdom:

Recall that patience is your faithful guide as you navigate the psychic terrain. Mastering psychic abilities requires accepting the baby steps of progress rather than sprinting to the finish line. Your psychic awareness grows with each encounter.

Your psychic abilities are nourished by patience, which makes them deep and robust.

Your Personal Haven:

You contain the center of psychic mastery. This inner sanctuary is a place of trust where you can connect with the limitless knowledge and insight buried deep inside of you.

You become the alchemist here, transforming the ordinary lead into the precious metal of psychic revelation.

Daily Alchemical:

The practice of developing psychic abilities transcends into daily existence. The everyday moments serve as the backdrop for your psychic exploration, so a grand stage is not necessary. You can find the extraordinary in these seemingly ordinary places—a chance meeting, a dream, a straightforward meditation.

The art of psychic mastery becomes a part of the ordinary and transforms life's canvas into a work of art.

The Heavenly Organ:

Your psychic abilities reveal a distinct melody like notes in an ethereal symphony. The symphony grows richer and more harmonious as you hone your abilities through practice. It is an endless composition, a work of art that is always changing.

You are the composer of the symphony that is your psychic journey, and with each note you play, you produce a masterpiece.

Permanent Rebirth:

Developing psychic abilities is a never-ending cycle of rebirth. You are reborn and evolve into a more perfected version of yourself with every insight and encounter. Your potential emerges from the cracks in the cocoon of limitation.

You release the limitations of the past and embrace the limitless horizons of the future with each rebirth.

Final Remarks:

As you close this chapter of your journey, keep in mind that you are still developing your psychic mastery. It is your ongoing magnum opus and the manifestation of your inner genius.

You improve the work of art that is your psychic journey with each new insight or revelation.

I hope you keep refining your psychic abilities with unwavering commitment and limitless curiosity. May you succeed in learning the truth—that the masterpiece isn't just your skills but the transformation of your very being—through your pursuit.

Accept the process and allow the process of becoming to be your ongoing work of art.

2. Leaning Into The Strength Of Community

The Third Eye does not require solitude as a condition for awakening. In actuality, a connection can serve as a lighthouse to help you navigate uncharted territory.

You'll find echoes of your own journey and the reassurance that you're not alone in the community of kindred spirits.

The search for souls with similar interests:

Being a psychic traveler, you have an exclusive journey. It is a natural yearning to connect with people who can relate to your experiences. Even though the journey is alone, the support of others helps.

You will find understanding mirrors in the eyes of those who share your vision.

Joining Spiritual and Psychic Communities:

You might find yourself drawn to spiritual and psychic circles in your search for a community. These societies are assemblies of souls traveling in parallel, each one adding a unique piece to the cosmic puzzle.

You'll find friendship, support, and a secure haven for your explorations within these circles.

The Link of Comparable Experiences:

You'll find the connection of shared experiences in the company of other seekers. Your lives are woven together by tales of psychic revelations, spiritual awakenings, and excursions into the metaphysical.

You'll find inspiration and a clearer understanding of your own path in these shared experiences.

An oasis of knowledge

Communities that are psychic or spiritual are rich environments where wisdom can flourish. Mentors, guides, and kindred spirits will be present to share their wisdom, experience, and insights with you.

These communities nurture the seeds of your personal psychic development, much like a garden of wisdom.

Welcoming Diverse Viewpoints:

You'll find a variety of viewpoints in these communities. Accept the differences, as it is from them that you will gain new perspectives, original methods, and a deeper comprehension of the mysteries of the Third Eye.

You'll find the vivid hues of your own awakening in the tapestry of various viewpoints.

The ripple impact:

Always keep in mind that your presence has an impact as you interact with a group of people who share your interests. Everyone's journey is made more meaningful by your experiences, wisdom, and insights that add to the collective consciousness.

You will discover through your interactions that you are a giver and a receiver, a teacher and a student.

Final Remarks:

May you find solace, motivation, and camaraderie on your journey along the Third Eye path as you seek out a group of like-minded people. Those who walk beside you enrich your journey, and you in turn enrich their journeys.

May your soul find a home in the embrace of your psychic tribe, and may your Third Eye keep awakening in the wisdom of community.

I hope that your relationships with other people provide you courage, wisdom, and a constant reminder that you are not alone in your search for the answers to the universe's mysteries.

3. The Way To Mastery: Developing Your Third Eye Esp Mastery

If you've made it this far, it's time to move on to the most exciting and last part of your journey: the quest for mastery. Not only is the Third Eye a skill, but it's a doorway to infinite wisdom and the knowledge of the universe's most profound mysteries. Are you prepared to master Third Eye ESP and realize all of its potential?

The Path to Mastery

The pursuit of mastery is a challenging yet attainable endeavor. It's available to anyone who is prepared to dedicate themselves to their own spiritual and personal development, not just a select group of people.

The road to mastery is paved with commitment, tenacity, and a resolute faith in one's own abilities.

Welcoming the Adventure:

Mastery is a lifelong journey, not a destination. It's the steadfast dedication to honing your skills, expanding your knowledge, and pushing the limits of your comprehension. The pursuit itself brings the real happiness.

You'll learn the Third Eye's mysteries along the way, and every revelation you make will motivate you to keep going.

An Inward Transformator:

You'll come to understand your function as an inner alchemist as you advance along the path to mastery. You'll turn intuition's basic components into insightful details. You will transform your ordinary perceptions into extraordinary revelations, much like an alchemist transforms lead into gold.

You will hone your skills and explore deeper levels of your own consciousness with each psychic experience.

Discover Your Inner Wise One:

Finding your inner sage is the key to mastery; it's not about acquiring external knowledge. Your psychic abilities are the tools that help you uncover this treasure, and your wisdom is within you.

You'll uncover the wisdom that has been waiting to be found in the silence of your thoughts.

Regular Exercise:

Mastery comes from daily practice. Set aside time for mindfulness, meditation, and psychic exercises. Your skills will be refined and tempered in this regular practice.

Every moment of practice is a step closer to mastery.

Learning from Others:

Mastery is not a solitary endeavor. Seek guidance from mentors and fellow travelers who have walked the path before you. They can offer insights, inspiration, and valuable guidance.

In the wisdom of others, you'll find the keys to unlock new levels of your own potential.

Final Remarks:

The path to mastery is not for the faint of heart, but for the courageous soul who believes in the magic within. It's for those who are ready to embrace their full potential and unlock the infinite possibilities of the Third Eye.

The journey to mastery is a journey to the heart of the cosmos, where you become the master of your own destiny.

May you embark on this path with zeal and unwavering commitment. In your pursuit of mastery, may you uncover the profound secrets of the Third Eye and inspire others to follow in your footsteps.

Embrace the journey, and let mastery be the legacy of your extraordinary psychic voyage.Inspiring and Teaching Others: Leaving a Legacy of Wisdom and Success

As you journey along the path of mastery in the realm of the Third Eye, it's not just your personal enlightenment that matters; it's also the impact you make on others. To become a beacon of inspiration and a teacher of wisdom is to leave a legacy that extends far beyond your lifetime.

4. Illuminating The Way For Others

Becoming a master of Third Eye ESP is a noble pursuit, but its true magnificence is in the sharing of knowledge and the illumination of others' paths. Here, we explore how you can inspire and teach, leaving behind a legacy of wisdom and success.

The legacy you create isn't etched in stone; it's woven into the very fabric of existence.

Lighting the Path:

Your mastery of the Third Eye is a torch that can light the way for others. It's about showing them that the extraordinary is within their grasp, that the mysteries of the universe are accessible.

Your light serves as an invitation for others to embark on their own journeys.

Passing on the Torch:

Teaching is a sacred act of passing on the torch of knowledge. Share your insights, experiences, and wisdom with those who seek to follow in your footsteps. As you teach, you deepen your understanding and refine your own abilities.

In teaching, you become both a guide and a student, a giver and a receiver.

Inspiring Awakening:

Your journey can be the catalyst for the awakening of others. Your story, your insights, and your mastery serve as an inspiration for those who are just beginning their exploration of the Third Eye.

Your journey is a living testament to the boundless potential of human consciousness.

Leaving a Legacy of Wisdom and Success

A legacy isn't built on wealth or possessions; it's created through the wisdom and insights you share. As you pass on your knowledge, you leave behind a profound legacy that enriches the lives of others.

Your legacy is a treasure trove of wisdom, an inheritance of insight for future generations.

Fostering Success:

Your mastery isn't just about psychic abilities; it's about fostering success in all aspects of life. Teach others to use their Third Eye for personal and professional growth, guiding them to achieve their dreams and aspirations.

Success is not just a destination; it's a journey guided by your inner vision.

Final Remarks:

As you approach the culmination of your Third Eye journey, remember that your legacy is a beacon of hope, a source of inspiration, and a testament to the unlimited potential of the human spirit. Your mastery isn't confined to your own being; it's a gift you bestow upon the world.

In the legacy you leave behind, you become a part of the grand tapestry of human evolution.

May you inspire and teach with boundless enthusiasm, and in doing so, create a legacy that will continue to inspire, guide, and enlighten generations to come.

Through your wisdom and success, you become a beacon in the vast sea of human consciousness, lighting the way for all who seek to explore the wonders of the Third Eye.

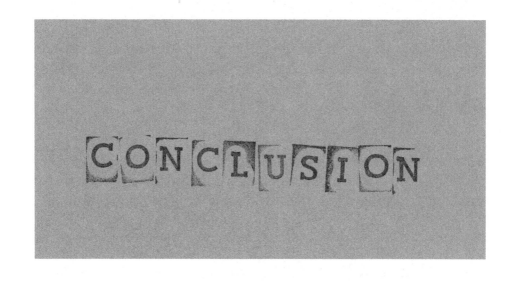

CONCLUSION:

The Power Of The Third Eye

In the journey to explore the power of the third eye, we have delved into the depths of self-awareness, intuition, and spiritual awakening. As we conclude, let's recap the key takeaways from this exploration and reflect on the ongoing transformation and success in your life.

Recap of the Key Takeaways:

1. Awakening Inner Wisdom: The third eye represents a source of inner wisdom, intuition, and perception beyond the physical senses. It offers a deeper understanding of ourselves and the world around us.

2. Meditation and Mindfulness: Practices like meditation and mindfulness are powerful tools for awakening the third eye. They help you quiet the mind, enhance intuition, and cultivate inner peace.

3. Intuitive Decision-Making: Trusting your intuition can lead to more informed and aligned decision-making. The third eye can guide you in making choices that resonate with your authentic self.

4. Spiritual Growth: Exploring the third eye often leads to spiritual growth and a deeper connection to the universe or a higher power. This journey can provide a sense of purpose and fulfillment.

5. Balancing the Chakras: The third eye is associated with the sixth chakra, but it's essential to maintain balance in all your chakras for holistic well-being.

The Ongoing Transformation and Success in Your Life:

The power of the third eye is not a destination but a continuous journey. As you continue to explore and develop this inner vision, you can experience ongoing transformation and success in various aspects of your life:

- **Personal Growth:** Embrace self-discovery and personal growth as you continue to unlock the potential of your third eye. It's a journey of lifelong learning and self-improvement.

- **Enhanced Perception:** Cultivate a heightened sense of perception that allows you to see the world with greater clarity. This enhanced awareness can lead to better relationships and improved problem-solving.

- **Intuition and Creativity:** Trust your intuition and tap into your creative potential. The third eye can be a source of inspiration for artistic and innovative endeavors.

- **Spiritual Fulfillment:** As your spiritual connection deepens, you may find a sense of purpose and inner peace that brings fulfillment and contentment to your life.

- **Empowerment:** The power of the third eye empowers you to navigate life's challenges with confidence and resilience. It's a source of strength and resilience in the face of adversity.

In conclusion, the journey to unlock the power of the third eye is a profound and transformative one. As you continue along this path, may it bring you increased self-awareness, wisdom, and success, leading to a life that is truly aligned with your deepest aspirations and desires. Remember that the journey never truly ends, and each step forward is a step toward a more enlightened and fulfilling existence.

EPILOGUE

As we approach the end of our study into the universe of the Third Eye, it is vital to reflect on the deep shift and awakening you've begun upon. Throughout this trip, we have dug into the depths of ancient Indian rituals and knowledge, harnessed the potential of extra-sensory perception, and examined the science and spirituality of the Third Eye.

You have toured the rich spiritual legacy of India, immersed yourself in the ancient disciplines of yoga and meditation, and mastered mindfulness methods that have opened doors to your inner awareness. You have learnt about the pineal gland, the chakras, and the awakening of the Kundalini energy, unleashing your intrinsic potential for spiritual enlightenment.

We have studied the worlds of clairvoyance, intuition, telepathy, telekinesis, and the extraordinary experiences of out-of-body adventures. You've been exposed to the techniques of remote viewing and astral projection, employing these powerful tools for personal and professional success.

Your path also spanned the areas of personal change, overcoming limiting beliefs, developing relationships, rising in your job, and increasing your general health and wellbeing. We've even ventured to dig into the darker elements of psychic ability, discussing ethical concerns and the hardships that may occur while treading this incredible road.

In the conclusion, we discussed the ethical use of Third Eye talents, the value of responsible psychic activities, and the relevance of assisting others while retaining your own integrity.

But remember, this is not the end of the road; it is only a milestone in your lifetime trip. Your Third Eye continues to emerge, and your psychic talents continue to grow. The ancient rituals and knowledge of India have given you the route, but the road is yours to travel. As you continue your adventure, you'll learn that mastery is a never-ending endeavor, and your legacy is the knowledge you share with the world.

In concluding, let us remember that the Third Eye is not only a notion or an idea; it is a source of unlimited potential inside you. The power of ESP, the insights into the universe's secrets, and the spiritual awakening are all at your fingertips.

Continue to embrace this adventure, to increase your knowledge, and to inspire others. Your life is a tribute to the possibilities of the human spirit. As you utilize your psychic skills for success, you add to a fabric of awareness that transcends time and place.

May your journey be filled with amazement, your heart with compassion, and your intellect with unending inquiry. The Third Eye is your guide, and the cosmos your painting. Keep painting the masterpiece of your life, and let it shine with the brightness of a thousand suns.

The voyage continues, and the options are unlimited. Awaken to your exceptional potential, because the cosmos awaits your next invention.

With unbounded gratitude and optimism,

~Mohd Faisal

ABOUT THE AUTHOR

Mohd Faisal

Mohd Faisal as an Indian author has penned several motivational books such as "The Ikigai Blueprints", "39 Commandments for Financial Success", and "Dark Triad Unmasked" etc. His books have helped thousands of readers across the globe to take control of their lives and achieve their dreams. His books offer practical advice and  actionable strategies for overcoming obstacles and achieving success in all areas of life.

His unique perspective and engaging writing style have earned him a loyal following of readers who appreciate his practical approach to personal growth and financial management. His books are an invaluable resource for achieving your goals.

BOOKS IN THIS SERIES

Ultimate ESP & Yoga Guide Collection

The "Ultimate ESP & Yoga Guide Collection" is a collection of inspirational publications that will lead you on a comprehensive path of self-discovery and wellbeing.

"Unlocking the Third Eye of ESP: A Journey into Expanded Perception and Kozyrev Mirrors" is a transformative book that explores the mysteries of Kozyrev Mirrors, extrasensory perception (ESP), and human consciousness. It provides insights into the Third Eye, its experiential, spiritual, and scientific aspects, and how opening it can lead to personal development and a deeper connection to one's surroundings. The book offers practical advice and real-world examples to enhance ESP abilities and personal growth.

"ESP Mastery: Boost Your Psychic Abilities and Awareness" is a comprehensive book that delves into Extra Sensory Perception (ESP), offering a balanced scientific approach. It provides practical exercises, clear guidance, and new perspectives on psychic abilities. The book incorporates the latest research, explores the mind-body connection, and emphasizes ethical practices. It is a transforming journey into personal growth and awareness, unlocking the limitless potential of the human mind.

"Kundalini Yoga Codes": Unlock Kundalini Yoga's secrets with this insightful manual. Discover the potent methods and practices that may harmonize your mind, body, and soul while awakening your spiritual energy.

"Anti-Aging Yoga": With the knowledge of "Anti-Aging Yoga," age gracefully and exude energy. Learn reviving postures, breathing techniques, and lifestyle advice that promotes longevity, increases flexibility, and fosters a young spirit. Accept the healing potential of yoga to care for your body and slow the passage of time.

"Chair Yoga Handbook" is an inclusive manual that encourages elders and those with physical disabilities to benefit from yoga's amazing health advantages. From the comfort of your chair, you may increase flexibility, build physical strength, and achieve inner calm with gentle postures, mindful practices, and adaptable sitting positions.

Take a journey of transformation with the "Ultimate Yoga Guide Collection." Each book provides relevant ancient wisdom, professional advice, and useful approaches. These books provide useful techniques to nourish your wellbeing and improve your life, whether you're a novice or a seasoned yogi.

By making an investment in yourself, you may realize your potential for development on the inside. Take use of yoga's capacity to lead a well-balanced life. Grab a copy of the "Ultimate Yoga Guide Collection" and get started right now!

Kundalini Yoga Code: Activating Your Kundalini Energy With Ancient Indian Kundalini Yoga.

Are you prepared to crack the code and release your inner strength? Discover yourself, your spirituality, and your deep energy by diving into the transforming realm of Kundalini Yoga.

About the Book:

In "Kundalini Yoga Code: Activating Your Kundalini Energy with Ancient Indian Kundalini Yoga," you'll set out on a road that fuses conventional knowledge with cutting-edge methods to awaken the latent power within of you. The holy practices, rituals, and teachings of Kundalini Yoga, a deep, age-old Indian discipline that may help you realize your fullest potential and awaken your latent Kundalini energy, are all covered in this thorough book.

Key features:
Discover the Ancient Wisdom: Learn about the Kundalini Yoga's rich history and background, which can be traced back to ancient India. Learn about the deep lessons taught by this transforming technique and its applicability in the modern world.
Kundalini Energy Activation: Discover potent methods and detailed practices to awaken and control your Kundalini energy. Discover a variety of Kundalini Yoga kriyas, breathing techniques, mantras, and meditations that are intended to awaken and balance your inner life force.
Discover the limitless potential that resides inside and experience a profound spiritual awakening to unlock your highest potential. Develop self-awareness, enlarge your consciousness, and amp up your vitality.
Healing and Transformation: Discover Kundalini Yoga's healing potential as you learn to clear blockages, purify your energy centers, and bring harmony and balance back to your physical, mental, and spiritual selves. Investigate the fundamental relationship between spiritual change and Kundalini energy.
Integrate Kundalini into Your Daily Life: Learn doable methods to integrate Kundalini Yoga into your daily schedule so that you may reap the rewards of this life-changing discipline in all facets of your existence. Learn how to incorporate Kundalini energy and awareness into your relationships, work, and everyday activities.

Unleash the Power Within:

Unlock the code that has been kept secret inside of you for a long time. The book "Kundalini Yoga Code: Activating Your Kundalini Energy with Ancient Indian Kundalini Yoga" is a step-by-step guide to waking up the latent energy inside of you, raising your awareness, and forging a powerful bond with the divine. Take this transforming journey and let Kundalini Yoga's boundless power flow through you.

Are you prepared to unlock the ancient Kundalini Yoga mysteries? Grab a copy of "Kundalini Yoga Code" and start reading to experience deep change, spiritual awakening, and self-discovery. The moment has come to awaken your Kundalini energy and reach your full potential.

The Anti-Aging Yoga Handbook : Ancient Indian Yogic Asanas For A More Youthful You

Are you trying to find a natural way to feel younger, more vibrant, and more energized?
Check out The Anti-Aging Yoga Handbook right away!

Using the power of yoga to counteract the effects of aging on the body and mind, this thorough book leads you on a step-by-step path to a more youthful self. This book has lots to offer whether you're an experienced yogi or a total novice.

You'll find a wealth of knowledge about yoga's anti-aging advantages within, along with a comprehensive guide to the best postures, breathing exercises, and meditation methods for regaining your youth and vigor. Clear directions, practical advice, and lovely graphics are all included in every chapter to aid you along the way.
But this book is more than just a practical guide to yoga. It's a friendly and engaging companion that will inspire you to embrace a healthier and happier lifestyle. You'll learn how to cultivate a positive mindset, reduce stress and anxiety, and improve your overall well-being.

So if you're ready to feel more youthful, energetic, and alive, don't wait another day. Pick up The Anti-Aging Yoga Handbook and start your journey to a more youthful you today!

Unlock Third Eye Of Esp: A Journey Into Esp And Kozyrev Mirrors

Are you prepared to set out on a transformative adventure that digs into the mysteries of Kozyrev Mirrors, extrasensory perception (ESP), and the depths of human consciousness?
Look nowhere else! The intriguing book "Unlocking the Third Eye of ESP: A Journey into Expanded Perception and Kozyrev Mirrors" will lead you on a life-changing voyage of self-discovery, expanded perception, and infinite potential.

Discover the Unseen:

Discover the secrets of the Third Eye, a doorway to expanded awareness, clairvoyant insights, and altered states of consciousness, in this ground-breaking book. Learn about the experiential, spiritual, and scientific facets of ESP and how opening your Third Eye can result in profound personal development and a deeper sense of connectedness to your surroundings.

The Kozyrev Mirrors Connection:

Examine Nikolai Kozyrev's avant-garde creations and his revolutionary theory of reflecting space-time. Learn how Kozyrev Mirrors, influenced by his ground-breaking theories, can be used as tools for entering altered states and examining the structure of reality. You'll discover how to build and use these mirrors to improve your ESP talents and explore unexplored areas of perception through engaging research, case studies, and hands-on activities.

Your Path to Transformation:

A fully immersive experience that inspires you to venture beyond the ordinary and into the extraordinary, "Unlocking the Third Eye of ESP" is more than just a book. Learn how to use practical methods to open your Third Eye, enter altered states of awareness, and communicate with invisible realms of existence. Discover the timeless wisdom that has guided seekers for generations as you navigate the complexities of ESP, explore the power of meditation, and learn more.

Why Choose This Book?
Exploration in depth: Learn about ESP, Third Eye activation, and the revolutionary ideas behind Kozyrev Mirrors.
Scientific and Spiritual Integration: Take advantage of a well-rounded strategy that integrates knowledge from the sciences with spiritual considerations to provide a wholistic viewpoint.
Practical Advice: To improve your ESP talents and perception, work through activities that are practical, followed by detailed instructions and real-world examples.
Personal Transformation: Set out on a path of self-discovery, inner development, and heightened awareness that will fundamentally alter the way you see the world and yourself.

Embark on Your Journey Today:
The book "Unlocking the Third Eye of ESP" is your ticket to a world of exceptional perception, profound understanding, and boundless possibilities. This book presents a guide for your voyage into the unexplored regions of human consciousness, whether you're a curious explorer, a spiritual seeker, or someone trying to tap into hidden realms of existence.

Don't pass up this chance to alter your perception and harness the Third Eye's power. Step into a world of limitless possibilities by ordering a copy of "Unlocking the Third Eye of ESP: A Journey into Expanded Perception and Kozyrev Mirrors" right away!

Esp Mastery: Boost Your Psychic Abilities And Awareness.

Unlock the Extraordinary Within You: ESP Mastery: A Book Unlike Any Other

"ESP Mastery: Boost Your Psychic Abilities and Awareness" serves as a beacon of enlightenment in a world where curiosity knows no boundaries and the hunt for the unusual beckons. This is more than a book; it is a transforming trip into the depths of human potential.

Why Should You Choose This Book Over Others:

1. thorough Insight: "ESP Mastery" is a thorough book that delves into the intriguing world of Extra Sensory Perception (ESP). It doesn't just skim the surface; it goes deep into the subject, providing you with a comprehensive comprehension of psychic phenomena.

2. Scientific Approach: In contrast to many other works on the subject, "ESP Mastery" adopts a balanced approach, mixing old knowledge with current science. It links the magical and intellectual worlds, offering a firm platform for your investigation.

3. Practical Exercises: This book isn't only about theory; it's also about doing. You'll be able to actively develop and improve your psychic talents via a variety of hands-on activities and procedures. "ESP Mastery" is your dependable companion on your path to self-discovery.

4. Clarity and Guidance: Written in an easy-to-understand style, this book provides guidance that even newbies to the realm of ESP

may grasp. It simplifies and manages difficult topics by demystifying them.

5. New Perspectives: "ESP Mastery" offers a unique viewpoint. It mixes old wisdom with current ideas to provide a comprehensive understanding of psychic talents. Whether you're a beginner or a seasoned practitioner, you'll discover fresh ideas and techniques to try.

What new in "ESP Mastery"?

Current Research: This book incorporates the most recent findings and research in the subject of psychic phenomena, guaranteeing that you have access to the most current knowledge.

Mind Body Connection: "ESP Mastery" explores the relationship between your mind, body, and psychic skills. It delves into the transformative power of mindfulness, meditation, and holistic wellness techniques on your ESP journey.

Ethical Exploration: The book highlights ethical practices and the responsible use of your newly acquired skills. It teaches you how to handle the nuances of ESP while maintaining your integrity and respect for others.

"ESP Mastery" is your key to unlocking the remarkable within you in a world where curiosity and the desire for selfdiscovery are celebrated. This book is about personal growth, awareness, and the limitless potential of the human mind, not only psychic talents. Explore the unexplored world of your own psyche and uncover your dormant talents.

Chair Yoga Handbook: A Practical Guide To Wellness And Well-Being.

The "Chair Yoga Handbook: A Practical Guide to Wellness and Well-being" will show you a new way to achieve wellbeing and well-being. This ground-breaking book provides a reviving method of yoga that is suitable for anybody, regardless of age, degree of fitness, or physical restrictions.

As you read through the pages of this extensive manual, immerse yourself in the practice of mindful movement. The "Chair Yoga Handbook" delivers the transforming power of yoga right to your seat, making it ideal for anyone looking for the advantages of yoga without the need for challenging poses or demanding practices.

Key Features:
Chair-Centric Practice: Gain knowledge about how to use yoga's therapeutic properties while relaxed and seated. Learn a variety of positions and exercises that will enhance your flexibility, strength, and balance.
Breath and Relaxation: Learn the skill of mindful breathing and relaxation methods that help improve your general sense of calm and focus while reducing stress.
Discover adapted yoga positions that energize and engage your body, promoting a healthy lifestyle even in the middle of a hectic schedule.
Mind-Body relationship: As you set out on a path to self-awareness, self-acceptance, and self-care, get a better knowledge of the mind-body relationship.
Inclusive Wellness: Everyone should read this book! "Chair Yoga Handbook" invites you to a complete and inclusive health experience, regardless of whether you're a senior trying to keep active, a professional seeking office-friendly stress reduction, or someone managing physical restrictions.
Expert Advice: Written by seasoned yoga practitioners, this guide blends the knowledge of traditional yoga with contemporary views to provide a thorough and useful resource.

The "Chair Yoga Handbook" can help you turn your daily routine into a health haven. Discover the joy of exercise, the calmness of mindfulness, and a healthier, more centered version of yourself. This book will lead you toward a better, more vivid life whether you are a novice or an expert yogi.

One seated pose at a time, rediscover the extraordinary potential your body is capable of. Embrace yoga's overall advantages with the help of the "Chair Yoga Handbook: A Practical Guide to Wellness and Well-Being." Here is where your path to a happier and more balanced life begins. The "Chair Yoga Handbook: A Practical Guide to Wellness and Well-being" will show you a new way to achieve wellbeing and well-being. This ground-breaking book provides a reviving method of yoga that is suitable for anybody, regardless of age, degree of fitness, or physical restrictions.

As you read through the pages of this extensive manual, immerse yourself in the practice of mindful movement. The "Chair Yoga Handbook" delivers the transforming power of yoga right to your seat, making it ideal for anyone looking for the advantages of yoga without the need for challenging poses or demanding practices.

~ THE END ~